Hope

THE ART OF LIVING SERIES

Series Editor: Mark Vernon

From Plato to Bertrand Russell philosophers have engaged wide audiences on matters of life and death. *The Art of Living* series aims to open up philosophy's riches to a wider public once again. Taking its lead from the concerns of the ancient Greek philosophers, the series asks the question "How should we live?". Authors draw on their own personal reflections to write philosophy that seeks to enrich, stimulate and challenge the reader's thoughts about their own life.

Clothes *John Harvey*
Commitment *Piers Benn*
Death *Todd May*
Deception *Ziyad Marar*
Distraction *Damon Young*
Faith *Theo Hobson*
Fame *Mark Rowlands*
Forgiveness *Eve Garrard and David McNaughton*
Hope *Stan van Hooft*
Hunger *Raymond Tallis*
Illness *Havi Carel*
Me *Mel Thompson*
Middle Age *Christopher Hamilton*
Money *Eric Lonergan*
Pets *Erica Fudge*
Science *Steve Fuller*
Sport *Colin McGinn*
Wellbeing *Mark Vernon*
Work *Lars Svendsen*

Hope

Stan van Hooft

Routledge
Taylor & Francis Group

LONDON AND NEW YORK

First Published 2011 by Acumen

Published 2014 by Routledge
2 Park Square, Milton Park, Abingdon, Oxon OX14 4RN
711 Third Avenue, New York, NY 10017, USA

*Routledge is an imprint of the Taylor and Francis Group,
an informa business*

Notices
Practitioners and researchers must always rely on their own
experience and knowledge in evaluating and using any
information, methods, compounds, or experiments described
herein. In using such information or methods they should be
mindful of their own safety and the safety of others, including
parties for whom they have a professional responsibility.

To the fullest extent of the law, neither the Publisher nor the
authors, contributors, or editors, assume any liability for any
injury and/or damage to persons or property as a matter of
products liability, negligence or otherwise, or from any use or
operation of any methods, products, instructions, or ideas
contained in the material herein.

ISBN: 978-1-84465-260-0 (pbk)

British Library Cataloguing-in-Publication Data
A catalogue record for this book is available from the British Library.

Typeset in Warnock Pro.

Hope is definitely not the same thing as optimism. It is not the conviction that something will turn out well, but the certainty that something makes sense, regardless of how it turns out.

Václav Havel

Surely political hope is always somehow utopian; it is a hope that we will set up a better world and set it up to endure. That must be true of every kind of political hope: that the situation could be different for good.

Alphonso Lingis

To a freedom fighter, hope is what a life belt is to a swimmer – a guarantee that one will keep afloat and free from danger.

Nelson Mandela

Providence has given human wisdom the choice between two fates: either hope and agitation, or hopelessness and calm.

Yevgeny Baratynsky

Hope is always the hope of being fulfilled, but what keeps the hope alive and so keeps the being open and on the move is precisely its unfulfillment. One may say that the paradox of hope (and the paradox of possibility founded in hope) is that it may pursue its destination solely through betraying its nature.

Zygmunt Bauman

What is Hope? Nothing but the paint on the face of Existence; the least touch of truth rubs it off, and then we see what a hollow-cheeked harlot we have got hold of.

Lord Byron

When Descartes said, "Conquer yourself rather than the world", what he meant was ... that we should act without hope.

Jean-Paul Sartre

Contents

Acknowledgements		viii
Introduction: mapping the terrain		1
1.	Defining hope	11
2.	Being hopeful	48
3.	Hope in the clinic	66
4.	Hope and politics	81
5.	Hope and religion	102
	Epilogue: the virtue of hope	136
	Further reading	141
	Bibliography	145
	Index	149

Acknowledgements

Many of the ideas developed in this book emerged from a series of seminars that I conducted with my students at Deakin University as part of their third-year assessment requirements. On-campus students were required to attend classes in which discussion was conducted using the format of modern Socratic dialogue, while off-campus students contributed to an online blog. The topic in each case was "What is hope?" I am grateful to these students for their insightful contributions. I am grateful also to Deakin University, whose support enabled me to take the time to write the book and to travel to various academic centres in order to conduct seminars in which its ideas were tried out before a critical audience. Specifically, I acknowledge the contributions of participants in seminars I conducted in the philosophy department at the National University of Singapore, and at an organization called "LogicMills" in Singapore, at which we discussed my ideas on the relations between hope and religion and hope and politics. In particular I thank Professors Loy Hui Chieh, Chin Liew Ten, Brian Mooney and Mark Nowacki. I also appreciate the input of Professor Raphaël Liogier and his students, including Melchior de Borde, at the Institute for Political Science (IEP), Aix-en-Provence in France. An anonymous reviewer of an earlier draft also made critical but helpful comments. Last, I thank my wife, Lynne, and daughters, Christine and Kate, for their patience as I regaled them with my thoughts over the dinner table.

Introduction: mapping the terrain

There is not much written about hope these days. Perhaps it is not an attitude that there is much call for in an age of constant war, global poverty and threatening environmental catastrophe. When the future seems to promise nothing but disaster it is resilience rather than hope that is the virtue most needed in our time. However, in this book I shall argue that hope is not only an essential existential attitude for all of us but also, if it is realistic, an important virtue.

To speak of virtue is to speak of character traits and dispositions that help us to live life well. The person of courage, for example, is able to face difficulties that inspire fear in her and so to succeed in her projects. The generous person is able to overcome his tendency to selfishness and so helps those in need and wins the gratitude and respect of others. In these and many other ways a virtuous person is able to succeed in life in a way that a vicious person will not. Of course, this understanding of virtue ignores the ethical or moral norms that are often associated with that concept. Most people think of being virtuous as an ethical requirement whose value resides in moral goodness as such. One should not act generously in order to win the favour of others but because being generous is a good thing in itself. These people will say that my account is too pragmatic: too concerned with making a success of life and not concerned enough about being morally good. Ancient Greek philosophers solved this problem by suggesting that if we are morally virtuous, we will go on to make a success of our lives. In this way virtue and successful living would inevitably go together. But there are too many successful rogues in the world today to give much encouragement to this way of thinking. Perhaps a better approach is to say that, if it is true that being virtuous makes you successful in life, then we might have to define success differently from the wealth and social power that the rogues I am referring to seem to enjoy. Perhaps being virtuous will make us happy, where being happy is to be understood in deeper terms than just material wealth and sensual pleasure. In this book I shall suggest that the virtue of hope is indeed important for making a success of life, but that we should understand the relevant notion of success as involving happiness in a deep sense that I shall explain presently.

In order to understand hope as a virtue, and in order to lay out the themes that I shall discuss in this book, it will be of interest to review what a range of authors have said about it.

Aristotle

The most notable ancient philosophical discussion of virtue comes from the Greek philosopher Aristotle (384–322 BCE). He suggests that our basic aim in life is to achieve happiness, which he understands as the fulfilment of our capacities and abilities as human beings. It does not consist just in the satisfaction of our desires – especially our material and sensuous desires – but in doing things that are worth doing and doing them as well as we can. It follows from this that a virtue is any character trait, ability or disposition that helps us to act nobly and well. Notice that the word "well" here speaks to being effective and successful in what we do, while the word "nobly" speaks to the ethical values of acting honourably and in accordance with the moral norms that prevail in our society. So the ethical and pragmatic values that we thought might be in conflict are combined here in the notion of virtue.

But what does Aristotle say about hope? Unfortunately, he says very little. However, he does offer us a framework for understanding it. When Aristotle thinks of virtues that involve the emotions or desires, he suggests that a virtue is located in an appropriate, usually middle, position between two extremes: an extreme of too little or an extreme of too much of the relevant emotion. So in the case of courage, which is a virtue that involves the emotion of fear, he says that courage lies between the extremes of foolhardiness (not feeling enough fear in the face of danger) and cowardliness (feeling too much fear in the face of danger). Being courageous is feeling the appropriate amount of fear in the face of danger: an amount that allows you to face up to the danger and act decisively without being unmindful of the risks you face. I shall apply this schema to hope and hopefulness in the chapters that follow.

But Aristotle does not confine himself to virtues that relate to our emotions, desires and attitudes. He also speaks of virtues that relate to our thinking and to our knowledge. There are not only virtues that set standards for our emotional lives, but also virtues that set standards for our rationality. Chief among the latter is wisdom. But this group also includes understanding and practical ability, along with the habit of mind that does not accept ideas or proposals without considering relevant evidence and reasons. Anyone who believes something simply because someone else has told him to – especially if that someone else has little or no expertise on the matter – is showing a lack of intellectual virtue of this kind. Once again, Aristotle himself does not discuss hope as an intellectual virtue. However, I will be suggesting in this book that hope should be realistic, and this invites us to understand hope in Aristotelian terms as an intellectual virtue or skill. If hope needs to be realistic then there must be an appropriate assessment of the facts of the matter. Is what is hoped for possible? Is it attainable? What are the chances of success? How much luck will be involved in the outcome? What do I need to do to achieve what I am hoping for? All these questions require intelligent answers and thus require intellectual virtue. We must exercise judgement that is sensitive to the realities and risks of the situation and also to the values inherent in what is hoped for. We must balance the risks against those values and act decisively. Hope inspires such a stance and in this way constitutes an intellectual virtue linked to sound judgement.

Hope requires one to imagine and foresee various scenarios and to assess risk factors. It requires one to acknowledge the values that are involved in a situation. If I am taking risks or facing dangers, driven by the hope of an outcome, is the value of that outcome commensurate with the risks and dangers? Does that value make facing the risks and dangers worthwhile? If hope is a motivation or a spur to action, then it requires the kind of sensitive judgement and prudence that Aristotle identified as the most important of the virtues.

Thomas Aquinas

Thomas Aquinas (1225–74 CE) was one of the greatest philosophers and Christian theologians of the medieval period in Europe and it will be of interest to explore his ideas on hope. Aquinas has two discussions of hope in his monumental work, *Summa Theologica*: one as an emotion that motivates action and the other as a virtue. Aquinas distinguishes two kinds of "passions" or emotions. First, there are those that express our desire for, or aversion to, things: emotions such as love, joy, sorrow and hatred. These are reactions to what causes us pleasure or pain. And, second, there are those that respond to the difficulties facing us that stand in the way of our attaining what we desire: such as daring, fear, hope and the like. These latter emotions play a motivational role in our attitudes and actions and are therefore more active than the first group. These emotions fire us up to overcome the difficulties that stand in the way of what we desire, or to flee from them. They spur us on to action.

Aquinas says that hope presupposes desire – we hope just for those things that we desire – and he distinguishes hopes from desires and wishes by noting that hope must fulfil four conditions. First, it must be for something good (as opposed to fear, which is of something bad). Second, its object is in the future. Third, its object must be something arduous and difficult to obtain (which is how it differs from a desire or a wish). And fourth, this difficult thing must be something possible to obtain: for one does not hope for that which one cannot get at all. Accordingly, Aquinas defines hope as a movement of the appetitive power (that is, of desire) ensuing from the apprehension of a future good, difficult but possible to obtain. What causes hope is thinking that the desired future good is obtainable – which may be because one has the requisite resources, ability or strength, or because the circumstances are propitious – and what prevents hope is thinking that that good is unobtainable. One's experience of events in the past that make one think that the goal is possible can lead to hope, just as experience that suggests it is impossible will snuff it out.

Aquinas also discusses the opposites of hope. Hope comes into being when we think that a desired object is difficult but possible to obtain. Accordingly, when we think a desired object is unobtainable, we are not spurred to action to obtain it and we suffer despair, which is, in that sense, the opposite of hope. Another opposite of hope is fear. But fear is the opposite of hope in the sense that its object – something bad – is the opposite of the object of hope – which is something good.

Aquinas gives us a hint that there is an ethical dimension to hope when he says that young people and drunkards can be more hopeful than older or sober folk. He says this is true of young people because they have more of a future in front of them and they live more in the future than in the past. Moreover, they are full of spirit and easily spurred on to undertake arduous projects. As well, they are less experienced in life. They have not suffered many defeats and so their experience tells them that many things are possible. People under the influence of alcohol think in the same way. They are easily spurred on despite the difficulties that confront them, and they are unmindful of experiences that should warn them of the risks. Aquinas's observations here could be taken as an ethical warning. The conditions of youth and inebriation apply also to foolish and thoughtless people in that they attempt everything and are full of hope. It is for this reason that the Aristotelian structure of virtue should apply to this emotion. One should not be excessive in hope just as one should not be deficient. If one were deficient one would not be motivated to take any action in pursuit of an arduous goal, but if one were excessive one would rush in like a drunkard and fail.

These observations stem from Aquinas's discussion of hope as an emotion linked to action. But when he addresses the question of whether hope is a virtue, he does so in a theological context. His first point is that hope, considered as a virtue, is not a passion, but a habit of mind. As a passion, the object of hope is a future good, difficult but possible to obtain. This form of hope is a movement of the appetites: a desire or wish. But Aquinas is now speaking of hope as a habit of mind or, as later elaborations would have it, an act of will. What he means by this is that it is a disposition or a commitment based in our thinking. It is not an emotion but a rational stance. Aquinas defines a virtue as a person's habit of mind that helps that person attain his or her good. As a religious believer, he then asserts that God is a person's ultimate good. From these premises Aquinas concludes that, in so far as hope helps us attain God through God's assistance, it is indeed a virtue.

This introduction of God into the discussion may be a little surprising, but it can be understood in the context of Aquinas's profound religious beliefs. For example, Aquinas asserts that the proper and principle object of hope is eternal happiness. But because that happiness consists in our union with God, God becomes the object that hope seeks to attain. Aquinas even argues that people should not place hope (in his special theological sense) in each other. It is only God who can help us attain our final end: that of eternal happiness in heaven. We can, however, rely on each other and place trust in others as possible helpers in our quest for salvation. But the proper object of the virtue of hope is our salvation with God. It follows that hope, as Aquinas understands it, is inextricable from religious faith.

Aquinas goes on to distinguish religious faith from hope by saying that faith gives us the truth about God and is in that sense cognitive, while hope allows us to trust in God's help in attaining eternal happiness and is therefore more like an attitude. Faith must come first since we must believe in God before we can hope to come to his presence in eternal salvation. Having argued earlier that hope must be for something possible but difficult to obtain, he now applies this to salvation and says that we must first believe the object of hope – our salvation in God – to be possible before we can hope for it. In this way faith comes before hope and is necessary for it.

Immanuel Kant

Jumping ahead a few hundred years, we come to the father of modern Western philosophy, Immanuel Kant (1724–1804), who writes:

> The whole interest of reason, speculative as well as practical, is centred in the three following questions:
> 1. What can I know?
> 2. What ought I to do?
> 3. What may I hope?   (*Critique* A805/B833)

The first question gave rise to his major work, *The Critique of Pure Reason*, while the second generated as many as three important publications: *The Groundwork for the Metaphysic of Morals*, *The Critique of Practical Reason* and *The Metaphysics of Morals*. But the third question generated no major exploration except a number of speculations about morality and religion. Indeed, in the text from which this quotation comes, Kant immediately turns the third question into a moral issue by suggesting that it should be understood as: "If I act as I ought to do, what may I then hope?" In this way, what we hope for is seen as a reward for being good: a reward that may come to us in this life or that we may be given in an eternal life after death.

Kant says that while we all hope to be happy, the real issue is that we should be worthy of being happy. It is not enough to hope to enjoy the fruits of happiness; we should also deserve the happiness we enjoy. In this way our hope for happiness is tied to our moral standing and to our sense of justice. Hope is seen as the motivation for our moral quest for being worthy of happiness, whether in this life or in the next.

Positive psychology

Modern psychology seems to understand virtue – and, more specifically, the virtue of hope – in less moralistic terms and as tied to success in life. For example, Christopher Peterson and Martin Seligman, the creators of what is today known as "positive psychology", understand virtue as what they call "character strengths" that enable us to live our lives effectively and happily. They define hope as, "Expecting the best in the future and working to achieve it; believing that a good future is something that can be brought about" (Peterson & Seligman 2004: 30). This suggests that they see hope as a form of action as well as an expectation or a belief. But it is as a mindset that hope is most important. They understand hope as "a cognitive, emotional, and motivational stance toward the future", thereby embracing both the way we see the world and the way we feel about it. However, they do make some distinctions between the cognitive dimensions of hope – which relate to our beliefs and knowledge – and the emotional dimensions of hope – which relate to our feelings and desires – when they say "*Hope* seems more emotional than its cousins and *optimism* more purely expectational. *Future-mindedness* and *future orientation* imply an articulate theory about what the individual needs to do to get from here to there (from the present to the desired future)" (*ibid.*). This focus on action and on hope as a motivation makes their account very pragmatic. There is no hint of any moral values and the focus is almost exclusively on making a success of life's everyday projects. Future mindedness, for example, is displayed by planning and making provision for what lies ahead. As Peterson and Seligman put it, "People high in this character strength make 'to do' lists, use day planners, and wear wristwatches; they also balance their check-books – all these activities imply an orientation to the future" (*ibid.*: 570). There is not much reference to moral values here. This is more a matter of prudence than of ethics.

Peterson and Seligman also make much of the way that hope is tied to action as a motivation. They argue that "optimism leads to continued efforts to attain the goal, whereas pessimism leads to giving up". They also note a problem; namely, "an optimistic bias in risk perception" (*ibid.*: 577). What they mean by this is that a hopeful or optimistic person will be less likely to apprehend risks to their projects or, if they do apprehend them, to take them seriously. This means that they are less realistic and will engage in activities even in the face of evidence that the enterprise is risky or prone to failure, or will persist in those activities even when they seem to be unsuccessful. In the long term, such an attitude is clearly not conducive to success in life, although in cases where luck has favoured the bold, such people are often regarded as heroes.

My plan for this book

It is not my intention in this book to pursue the theological or moralistic paths opened up by Aquinas and Kant. I do not see hope as a fundamentally theological virtue or as an intrinsically moral motivation. What I will do is use an Aristotelian framework to add depth to the positive psychology account. I want to explore what hope is and what role it plays in our everyday lives as human beings. What can we learn about ourselves as human beings given that we are beings who hope? I shall claim that hope is a fundamental structure of the way we live our lives. It is a way of shaping how we view ourselves and the world in which we live. It is a structure of our identity. Whether we hope for a life after death or for good weather tomorrow – whether our hopes are grand or humble – hoping is part of our outlook on life. What we hope for defines who we are. This will have some ethical implications – some of our hopes might be silly or unrealistic and should therefore be put aside – but the most important reason for exploring hope is to understand ourselves better as human beings.

In this book I shall embark on this exploration by enquiring into what the concept of hope means in our everyday uses of the term. I shall then investigate the Aristotelian suggestion that being hopeful is part of a well-lived life: that is, that hope is a worldly virtue. After that I shall apply what we have learnt to three very different situations. The first of these is the medical clinic where a patient who is dying might be sustained by hope. I shall then turn to society and explore the role that hope plays in political engagement. Last, I shall return to the assumptions made by Aquinas and Kant and explore the connection between hope and religious faith, but it will be to suggest that our hopefulness creates such faith rather than that our faith sustains our hope. I shall end by espousing a realistic kind of hope that will be conducive to living a meaningful life and to attaining a fragile happiness.

1. Defining hope

What do we mean by "hope"? Hope seems to be a psychological state that we experience as part of our inner, subjective lives. However, not all usages of the word designate a state of mind in this way. We sometimes say of someone that "he does not have a hope". Suppose a goal kicker of average ability is taking a penalty kick against a team and a goalkeeper who are very skilled at football. As he is about to take his kick we might say of him that he has no hope of scoring the goal. We do not mean by this that he does not hope to score the goal. Indeed, we assume that he does hope to. But we are not referring to his psychological condition or to any mental states he might be in. We are referring to the objective fact that he has but a very slim chance of scoring a goal: so slim, in fact, that we think there is no likelihood at all that he will score a goal. We express this by saying that he has no hope of doing so. This statement is a description of the physical or factual likelihood of the outcome taking place. It is an assessment of the objective circumstances rather than of the internal psychological state of the footballer.

But the meaning that we are more interested in is when the word is being used to refer to the way someone feels or thinks about a situation. Let us explore this thoroughly.

An example

John has to go out to attend a lecture at his university and he doesn't have an umbrella. Moreover, he is moving house and so most of his clothes are in boxes and relatively inaccessible. The weather forecast says there is a chance of rain and John does not want to get wet. Not only would getting wet be uncomfortable, but if his clothes get wet he will have nothing to wear the next day. As he is about to leave his house the sky is clear, but he can see dark clouds forming in the distance. John hopes that it will not rain.

What conditions have to obtain for it to make sense for John to hope that it will not rain? What are the thoughts and feelings that John needs to have for it to be appropriate for us to use the word "hope" in describing his state of mind?

The first thing that seems to be necessary is that he has a relevant desire. Indeed, he has a number of relevant desires. He desires to get to his university and he desires to do so at a certain time (with the consequence that he cannot wait for the weather to clear up). These desires flow from his commitment to his university studies. But his most relevant desire is the desire not to get wet. He would not enjoy walking to his destination in the rain. Indeed, in this case it is an unusually urgent desire since he does not have a change of clothes readily available to him. Accordingly, getting his clothes wet would not only be uncomfortable but would also be a serious inconvenience. John desires not to suffer this inconvenience. Moreover, not only does he need to have a desire that it not rain, but he has to be worried about the effect that the rain would have on him if it should come. He has to give thought to the unfortunate consequences to him of getting wet. Unlike Gene Kelly in the famous scene from the film *Singin' in the Rain*, John is anxious not to get wet. It is a matter of concern to him that his clothes stay dry so that he can wear them again the next day. The weather forecast, along with his seeing the dark clouds in the distance, only increases his anxiety about the possibility of getting wet.

A second condition is a consequence of the first. This is that John must consider it to be a good thing for him if it does not rain. It might not be good for farmers or gardeners who need rain, but given John's needs and concerns, he will judge it to be a good thing if it does not rain.

A third condition that needs to obtain for it to make sense for John to hope that it will not rain is that he has to consider it to be possible that it will rain. If John were convinced that it would not rain, there would be no point in his hoping that it would not. This condition is fulfilled in the example because he has heard a weather forecast that predicts that it will rain and because he has seen the dark clouds gathering in the distance. Notice that this is a psychological matter. It is not the objective possibility that it will rain that is important but the fact that he considers it possible. There are meteorological conditions that make it more or less likely that it will rain, and a certain set of meteorological conditions obtains on that day. According to the weather report those actual conditions are such as to make it likely that it will rain. On other days they might have been such as to make it very unlikely, if not impossible, that it would rain. These are objective conditions that are as they are irrespective of what John or anyone else thinks about them. What we are considering in the example, however, is what John considers possible or likely. One could imagine that if John were going out on a day when rain was extremely unlikely, he might still hope that it does not rain. But if he does have such a hope it will be because he thinks that rain is possible. If he were convinced that it was impossible that it would rain, then it would make no sense for him to hope that it would not. He would then not need to have such a hope because he already knows that it will not. But in this example he is envisaging an unwelcome possibility, that it will rain, and hoping that it will not eventuate. For him to hope that it will not happen he must consider it to be possible that it will.

A fourth condition for its making sense for John to hope that it will not rain is that it is possible that it will not rain. What this means is that if John knew that the meteorological conditions were such that rain was inevitable, then it would make no sense to describe John as hoping that it would not rain. If he hopes that it does not rain he must consider it possible that it does not rain. It follows that he must not think that rain is inevitable. If the conditions and indications were such as to induce in John the belief that rain was inevitable, it would make no sense for him to hope that it does not rain. This would be especially clear if we imagine John leaving the house when it is already raining. It certainly would not make sense for him then to hope that it does not rain. The technical term to describe the third and fourth conditions together – that the hoped-for event is possible but not inevitable – is the word "contingent". An occurrence is contingent if it might or might not have happened: that is, if it was not necessary, inevitable or impossible that it should happen. An occurrence is contingent if luck – in the form of unknown or unexpected causal influences – can intervene to make it happen or to stop it from happening.

The role of time in these conditions leads me to propose a fifth. As we have just noted, if John were to step outside and feel the rain on his skin it would make no sense for him to say "I hope it does not rain". It would be even stranger for him to say "I hope it is not raining". If it manifestly is raining, to say such a thing would be to misuse the word "hope". He might say "I wish it were not raining", but he could not say "I hope it were not raining". John's thought "I hope it does not rain" refers to the future. It might be more accurate to convey its content by saying "I hope it will not rain" and in this way make the future reference of the hope more explicit. But it is interesting to reflect that, from John's own point of view, anything is possible in the future. Even if the meteorological conditions were such that rain was completely inevitable, the fact that the rain is not yet actual gives John the psychological possibility of thinking that it might not come and hence of hoping that it will not. On the other hand, if time has passed so that that envisaged future is already settled, what was in John's future has become the present or the past. Accordingly, it will no longer be considered possible for things to turn out differently from the way they have. If the rain has started, it is no longer possible that it not be raining. It follows that it would make no sense for John to hope that it will not rain. If it ever does make sense to say "I hope it is not raining" when it actually is raining, we could imagine it doing so when John does not know whether it is raining as he is about to leave the house. In this case his hope is future oriented in his thinking if not in fact. What is objectively the case in the present is indeed the case. It is either raining or it is not. But John does not know whether it is. He will find out as soon as he steps outside. His stepping outside is still in the future, however, and so it makes sense for him to hope that it is not raining. In this case, he is hoping that what he finds out about the weather when he steps outside is that it is not raining.

What we have learnt from this example is that hopes are oriented toward the future. Suppose it had rained yesterday and that John had been out in the rain and his clothes had become wet. This had been a discomfort and inconvenience to him. Would it make sense for him now to hope that it had not rained yesterday? No, it would not. If it happened yesterday then he cannot now hope that the circumstances had been different. We saw above that it only makes sense to speak of hope if what is hoped for is possible. But yesterday's weather cannot be different now from what it was. It has happened in the past and cannot now be changed. That it did not rain yesterday is therefore impossible now. And if it is impossible, John cannot be said to hope for it.

This is not to say, however, that John cannot have some kind of feeling towards yesterday's weather that is, perhaps, similar to hope.

He can wish that it had not rained yesterday, just as he can wish that it were not raining now when it actually is. The conditions for making sense of this are similar to the conditions that make sense of hope. He has a desire that it does not rain and that he does not get his clothes wet. And, in light of the science of meteorology, it is objectively possible that it might not have rained yesterday, even though, in fact, it did. But it is not now possible that it will not have rained yesterday because, in fact, it did. The feeling that John can have today that is similar to hope but different from it, is that he can wish that it had not rained yesterday.

A wish is a psychological state that is similar to a hope in interesting ways. Both are expressions of what John wants and of what he is anxious about. John wants to walk outside without getting wet and is anxious about ruining his clothes. He expresses this by feeling and articulating various wishes and hopes. With reference to the future he hopes that it will not rain, while with reference to the past he wishes that it had not rained. Hope refers to the future while, in this case, John's wish refers to the past. As I noted above, he could also wish that it were not raining in the present. If it is actually raining now, he could wish that it were not. But he cannot be said to hope that it not raining when it actually is raining since that would be hoping for something that, given present meteorological conditions, is never going to happen. Hopes can only refer to what is possible in the future.

Of course, wishes can refer to the future also. Let us imagine that when John steps outside and sees the dark clouds gathering he becomes convinced that rain is inevitable. He now considers it impossible that it will not rain. Accordingly, the fourth condition for its making sense for him to hope that it will not rain is not met. If he is completely convinced that it will rain, he cannot hope that it will not. Nevertheless, it would make sense to say of him that he wishes it would not rain. Even if he were to feel the first drops of rain on his clothes, he could go on wishing that it would not rain.

His wishes can extend into the future and embrace any scenario. His hopes, however, are limited to what is possible, and if it is actually raining then it is no longer possible that it is not raining now. Accordingly, he cannot hope that it does not rain.

We can describe this difference between hopes and wishes in more general terms. We could say that wishes do not need to be realistic while hopes do. Just how realistic hopes should be is a matter we shall explore later. For the moment it is important to see that wishes need not be realistic at all. Not only can John wish that it not rain even when it manifestly is raining, but he can also wish that it had not rained yesterday when it clearly did. More generally, John can wish that the tooth fairy will stop it from raining or that the Easter bunny will bring him good luck. He can wish that global warming was not a reality or that dire poverty in the developing world was not the cause of millions of avoidable deaths every year. He can wish that he was rich or a champion footballer. In short, he can wish for the realization of any of his fantasies, the alleviation of all his anxieties, the satisfaction of all his desires and the fulfilment of all his ideals. But he can only hope for what he considers possible.

A sixth condition is implicit in what we have seen already. Given that it might or might not rain and that John does not know whether it will, we could say that he is uncertain about whether it will rain. Whether it will rain or not is an objective matter. Given the meteorological conditions and the laws of nature, it will either rain or it will not. The occurrence of rain is objectively contingent. But corresponding to this objective state of affairs there is the subjective state of John's not knowing whether it will rain or not. He is uncertain about the weather. It is this uncertainty, together with his anxiety about not getting wet, that leads him to hope that it will not rain.

There is also a seventh condition. Suppose John had an umbrella. We have already noted that he wants to keep dry when he goes outside and that he is anxious about getting his clothes wet. Let us qualify this a little by saying that he wants to keep relatively dry, or as dry as using an umbrella would make him. If this were what he wanted and if he had an umbrella, then it would be within his power to secure what he wants and allay his concerns when he goes outside in the rain. He just needs to put up his umbrella. In this circumstance, does it make sense for him to hope that it will not rain? Perhaps this question will gain more focus if we reformulate it as: would he hope that he will not get wet? (It was, after all, because he did not want to get wet that he hoped it would not rain in the original scenario.) I think it would not make very much sense for him to hope that he would not get wet because he has it within his power to ensure that he does not get wet. He only has to put up his umbrella. If he can control his circumstances in such a way as to avoid an unpleasant outcome or to secure a pleasant outcome, then it makes little sense for John to merely hope for that outcome. Rather, his mental state should be that of intending to secure that outcome. He could just go ahead and do what was necessary. To say that he hopes for that outcome implies that he cannot control all the parameters of the situation so as to secure the outcome he wants. To say that John hopes that he will not get wet implies that he cannot control whether or not he gets wet. If he can control it by using his umbrella, then it would be redundant for him to also hope not to get wet. (Once again, however, he could still wish that he not get wet, even as he is putting up his umbrella. The notion of a wish seems much more accommodating.)

To return to the original example in which John did not have an umbrella, we can apply this point by suggesting that a further condition for its making sense for John to hope that it would not rain is that he has no control over whether it rains or not. This point is easily missed in this example because no one has any significant control over meteorological conditions. The forces of nature that are involved here are too great and amorphous to admit of human control (although climate scientists do hope that there are things human beings can do to reduce the effects of global climate change). It is certainly true that no one can control whether it will rain today, least of all John himself. It is because he knows that he cannot control whether it rains or not that it makes sense for him to hope that it will not rain. If he were to be able to control the weather he would not need to hope for that outcome: he could just do what was necessary to secure it.

Let us summarize, then, the conditions that make it appropriate for John to hope that it does not rain in the circumstances I have described.

1. John has to be concerned about the effect of rain on him. This applies because he has a desire not to get wet.
2. John has to consider that it would be a good thing for him if it did not rain. (This follows from the first condition.)
3. He has to consider that it is possible that it will rain.
4. He has to consider that it is possible that it will not rain: that is, that rain is not inevitable.
5. The hope is directed towards weather conditions that lie in John's future.
6. John is uncertain about whether it will rain.
7. John is not able to control the meteorological forces that would stop it from raining.

Do these conditions allow us to offer a definition of what hope is? They certainly give us some clues as to what clauses should appear in such a definition.

Hopes and wishes

While discussing our example we had occasion to contrast hopes and wishes. Let us therefore begin our task of defining hope by specifying what features hopes have that wishes do not have. What we discovered earlier is that a hope is a wish that differs from other wishes in that its object needs to be considered to be in the future of the person who is hoping for it, that the person who is hoping for it cannot bring it about entirely by her own efforts and that it is possible that what is hoped for could occur or could not occur. While some of these features apply to wishes as well, not all of them do. Most notably, a wish can be for something that is not possible, either because it is in the past or because the laws of nature will not allow it to happen. I would suggest that this is a definitive difference between hopes and wishes. A hope should be for something that is possible.

What other differences might there be between wishes and hopes? It is sometimes suggested in popular films for children that if you wish for something hard enough it will come to you. This point suggests that wishes admit of degrees: that you can wish in a more or less intense manner. Does hope admit of degrees in this way? If it did then hope would share this property with other emotions. You can be more or less angry and you can be more or less sad. While it might be naive to say that if you just hope hard enough what you hope for will happen, it does seem to make sense to speak of hoping more or less intensely. One way in which this would make sense is that one can desire what one hopes for more or less intensely. John's desire that his clothes not get wet is fairly intense because getting them wet would be seriously inconvenient for him. He is worried about getting his clothes wet. However, it is not a life or death matter. His hope is intense to the degree that his desire and his concern not to get wet are intense. Moreover, it seems we could say that the intensity of hope is inversely proportional to the likelihood of the hoped-for event occurring. If John thinks that it is very unlikely that it will rain, then he does not have to hope so intensely that it will not. His hope will be tempered by his expectation. In contrast, if he notes the dark clouds and the weather report and thus thinks that rain is very probable, his hope that it will not rain will possibly be more intense.

However, before we accept the idea that hope admits of degrees, we should notice that it is not easy to imagine what a more intense hope would feel like in contrast to a less intense hope. There do not seem to be qualitative, experiential features in hopes that allows us to measure their intensity in the way that there is with anger or sadness. One can feel more or less angry, but can one feel hope more or less intensely? It would seem not. Perhaps this shows that hope is not an emotion in any simple sense. If we do speak of John hoping more or less intensely, we might be speaking obliquely about his desire that it will not rain and his anxiety about the consequences of the rain for him and suggesting that *they* can be more or less intense. The desire, the anxiety and the hope are inextricable from each other and so the intensity of the former rubs off on the latter.

There might also be further ways in which hopes differ from wishes. We might, for example, suggest that hopes differ from wishes in that they are more serious. The wish that Santa Claus brings me a Christmas present might be thought to lack serious-ness in this sense. Not only is this a wish for something impossible in that it refers to a person who does not exist, but it also seems somewhat childish or frivolous, rather than reflecting a serious engagement with life and its challenges. It might help to use a more serious example to make this point. One of my students – let us call her Fatima – is a mother who has had the heart-wrenching experi-ence of having one of her children go missing. The child was found soon after and was unharmed, but while it was lost Fatima suffered considerable anxiety. She hoped that her child would be found. It would sound too weak and inappropriate to say that she wished that her child would be found. The word "wish" lacks the seriousness, urgency and engagement with reality that this situation calls for. This suggests that wishes are indeed less serious than hopes.

However, I am not sure that this is a characteristic that would not also be found in hopes. In the less serious case, it still makes sense to describe a person as hoping that they will be given a present. Even if they do not refer to Santa Claus or any other unrealistic entity so that what is wished for becomes impossible, the hope might still be essentially flippant. If I hope to receive a new shaving kit for my birthday, or a newly reissued Miles Davis CD for Christmas, such a hope may be described as lacking in seriousness no matter how much I want those things or, as in the case of the shaving kit, need them. While it will not be easy to judge which things are serious and which are not, and thus which wishes are serious and which are not, it does seem possible to hope for things that are either serious or not. If this is so, seriousness – however we define it – will not be a feature that can serve to distinguish hopes from wishes. It does not seem inappropriate to describe someone as hoping for something flippant.

And yet there might be an important idea hiding within this suggestion. We noted in the first example that John had a concern about the weather. He was worried about his clothes getting wet and this anxiety, although it was mild, constituted a context that allowed us to understand his psychological state as one of hope. While it might not be a difference that distinguishes hopes sharply from wishes, it might be suggested that whereas hopes arise from concerns in this way and share in their intensity, wishes arise only from desires and fantasies. My wish that I receive a present is not driven so much by any concerns or worries that I might have as by my yearning for the things that I want. Not having the things I crave may be a source of some form of disquiet in me, but it would seem inappropriate to think of this as anxiety. I am not worried about some potential harm that might befall me, but just vaguely discontented or in a state of longing. It remains true, however, that I could respond to this longing either by hoping that I receive what I want or by wishing for what I want. The broader notion of a wish would seem to apply just as readily as the narrower notion of a hope. What would make the notion of hope appropriate so that I could describe myself as hoping for the present rather than as merely wishing for it, is if I feel an increased intensity of yearning marked by a degree of anxiety about not receiving it. Just wishing to receive it can be light-hearted, while hoping to receive it seems somewhat more urgent. If I hope to receive it, I am displaying some degree of anxiety about not receiving it.

The role of anxiety is more evident in the more serious case of Fatima and her lost child. This case suggests a link between hope and dread: that hope is the positive side, as it were, of anxiety. If we fear some bad outcome we can express that fear by dreading the bad outcome, by hoping for a good outcome, or both. Anxiety is fear that the worst can happen, while hope is a stance taken in the face of the fear that the worst can happen. Fatima hopes to find her lost child because she fears the alternative possibility: that the child is never found. Moreover, it is the uncertainty that pervades such times of crisis that generates both the anxiety and the hope. If there were no doubt that the child would be found, Fatima would feel but little anxiety and would not need to hope for that outcome. She would simply expect it. In this case there might be some impatience but there would not be nearly so much anxiety. It is when there is anxiety present that we speak of hope rather than a mere wish. And when we speak of hope as being intense we are suggesting that it is motivated by intense anxiety. Fatima knows this only too well. As we noted earlier, it would be too weak to say that she wishes to find her child since, while it is true that she desires to find her child, she also feels a high level of distress and fear about the child's welfare. Hopes differ from wishes, then, in that they are generated by a relatively high degree of anxiety or concern.

Wishes and hopes seem to have slightly different objects as well. Consider the locution "I wish I had a Miles Davis CD; I hope I'll get one soon". Here the two words "wish" and "hope" differ in that the wish seems to be a desire for a specific object, while the hope seems to be looking forward to an event that involves the fulfilment of the wish. The wish is for an object while the hope is that something will happen. Once again, however, I doubt that this distinction is sharp enough to be definitive. The broader notion of a wish could be used to describe what I hope will happen as well as what I desire to obtain, as in "I wish my wife would give me a Miles Davis CD". Nevertheless, wishes seem not to need specific events or occurrences as their objects. I may wish I were a millionaire but I hope to win the lottery. The wish is for a state of affairs, while the hope is that something will happen. Moreover, because hopes are for something that is possible, I must have purchased a lottery ticket if I am to be described as hoping to win. But I can wish I were a winner even without buying such a ticket and so without having any hope of winning. My wish has no foundation other than desire while my hope has some grounding in reality.

This suggests that another difference between a hope and a wish is the level of attainability of what is desired and the associated anticipation levels that result. Bob buys a lottery ticket and wishes that he would win. This wish has an element of frivolity to it because Bob knows that the chances of winning a major prize are vanishingly small. His wish loosens the grip of reality on him and allows him to dream a little. Perhaps the reason we have such wishes is that they allow us to escape from the pressures of daily life and to relax the harsh grip of reality. This may be psychologically important in allowing us to function in an otherwise uncompromising world. In buying a lottery ticket Bob is taking an easy – although unlikely – way out. Whereas he could work hard to gain the financial security he desires, he chooses to buy the lottery ticket instead. Rather than acting decisively and rationally, he relies on a slim chance of winning a fortune. The reason that we might think of this as frivolous is not only that the chances of winning are so small or that a fortune is not, in itself, such an important thing, but because Bob has chosen an easy option. He has not chosen to work harder but to gamble. It is the lack of a connection between appropriate action and the desired outcome that is characteristic of his wish.

This, in turn, suggests that a distinguishing characteristic that would mark off hopes from wishes is that there is a link between hope and appropriate action. A hope would be something we are willing to invest effort into. Such a connection between hope and action may be absent in the case of wishes. When we hope for something, it may be that we can do something to achieve it, no matter how effective it might be, whereas when we wish for something we simply wait to see if what we wish for comes about. A wish is often for something less attainable and as a result is accompanied by a feeling that there is nothing we can do to fulfil it. It is often based on circumstances out of our control, and so we put less, little or no effort into attaining it. With a hope, we are more likely to act on it, as it is closer to our grasp, and we invest more into it. Hope is appropriate for those who have some degree of control, and wishing is appropriate for those who do not. This explains why I can wish I would win the lottery even if I have not bought a ticket while I could not be described as hoping to win without a ticket.

Interestingly we can describe a situation as hopeless but we cannot describe it as wishless. Wishing is always an option. When we have no control over the situation at all, we are left only with wishing. If we are merely wishing for something, we are not actively pursuing whatever it is. We may even feel that it is unrealistic to do so. We may not be so fanciful as to expect Santa Claus to grant our wish, but we are not doing anything about it either. When we hope, there is an inclination to do whatever we can to attain the desired outcome, such as searching for the lost child, but we do so with the realization that we cannot control everything ourselves. Although hope implies some degree of control, it also implies limits to that control, as we noted earlier. At some stage we have to say that we have done all we can do and hope that the rest falls into place. We can only speak of hope when we are still holding on to some possibility, however slim, that what we want will happen.

Take the case of Christine Collins, the heroine in the film *Changeling*, played by Angelina Jolie. Her son, Walter, goes missing and is never found. It transpires that a depraved murderer has been kidnapping young boys and killing them on a remote farm. After some seven years one of the missing boys appears, but he is not Walter. He is David, who had known Walter on that farm. Although he did not see Walter being killed, everything he reports indicates that Walter is dead. Nevertheless, Christine, having seen David alive and having heard his story, says that she now has something that she did not have before: hope. When the odds of a good outcome in a situation become slimmer and slimmer we normally talk of "losing hope", or even of "all hope being lost", and yet Christine goes on hoping. Is this an admirable determination to never give up hope, or is this a case of "wishful thinking"? If there is nothing more that Christine can do, the link between hope and action is lost and it would seem more appropriate to describe her as wishing that her child be found. But if there is still something she can do, even if it is so minimal an action as scrutinizing boys she sees in the street, then she could truthfully say that she still hopes to find her child.

This last point seems to have added a new condition to the seven we found to be definitive of when it is appropriate for John to hope. John hopes that it would not rain but was not able to do anything that would secure that outcome. Yet we described him as hoping. On the other hand we have now suggested that using the word "hope" implies that the hoping person is doing, or is at least inclined to do, something to realize that hope. Perhaps it matters how we describe Christine Collins's hope. If she hopes that her child be found then she is hoping for an outcome of which she is not the agent. It is other people who will find the child or not. It is out of her hands. Nevertheless, this is a genuine case of hope because it fulfils the seven conditions and is more than just a wish. But if we describe her as hoping that she will find her child, we are implying that she is herself trying to find her child and that her hope is a function of her effort in doing so. If, after such a time that, objectively, all hope is lost, we can still say that she has not given up hope, we are suggesting that she has not given up trying. And we find this admirable.

Hope and action

Our attempts at distinguishing hopes from wishes have suggested a close link between hope and action, a link that is absent in the case of mere wishes. It is through action that we change the world so that it fits with our desires and hopes. If we want something we are motivated to do something to obtain it. Is it also the case that if we hope for something we are motivated to do something to obtain it? We have seen that if we wish for something we are not necessarily motivated to do something to obtain it because we may be engaged only in wishful thinking. So what about hope? We have discussed two examples that speak differently to this issue. John hoped that it would not rain. In his case there was nothing he could do to bring that eventuality about and so his hope did not lead to the kind of action that would stop it from raining. Christine Collins hoped that she might find her son. In her case there was something – albeit a very minimal something – she could do: be on the lookout for him. In the film she pursued this course of action even at the cost of missing social and possible romantic opportunities that came her way. In both cases it seemed appropriate to describe the relevant psychological state as one of hope. Is it, then, an essential element in hope that it leads to action or is a hope where no action is possible also a genuine case of hope? It seems that the relations between hope and action are complex.

One contemporary philosopher, Patrick Shade, defines hope as "the active commitment to the desirability and realizability of a certain end" (Shade 2001: 70). The first point inherent in this definition is that every action has an end or a goal. The second point is that the end or goal that we pursue must seem desirable to us. This does not entail that it must be pleasant, but we must see it as something that we want to achieve for some reason or other. It may be important or frivolous, morally required or morally neutral, pleasant or unpleasant, but we must have some cogent reason for pursuing it. We engage in an action in order to attain that goal. In cases where the goal is not impossible but difficult to reach because of some difficulty or obstruction we need strong motivation so that we are prepared to make the needed effort. We need commitment to our goal. According to Shade, hope is the form that this commitment takes. As he puts it, "hope has as its object an end (whether a thing or an event) whose realization lies beyond our present agency; that end may be remote or directly obstructed, yet insofar as we hope for it, we nevertheless remain committed to pursuing its realization" (*ibid.*: 3). He argues that our hopes sustain us when our ends do not seem realizable and that they are in that sense productive and expansive. This stress on commitment suggests that hope is an attitude towards the course of action that the agent is embarking on when that course of action includes difficulties and challenges. But Shade also speaks of "active" commitment. This suggests, in turn, that it is not just the attitude that is important but also the way we put that attitude into effect. Indeed, Shade goes so far as to define hope as an activity. As he puts it, "Hope is pragmatically conceived not as a private mental state, but as an activity belonging to an organism in dynamic relation with its environment. Hope, then, should be treated as an activity, as hop*ing*" (*ibid.*: 14).

But this account of hope as commitment and activity is problematic in John's example. John hopes that it will not rain, but there is nothing he can do to bring that state of affairs about. The problem here is that its not raining is not a goal of John's action. His goal is to get to university without getting wet. It not raining is a state of affairs that he is concerned should obtain, but it is not a goal that he can pursue. Not only can he not do anything to prevent it from raining, but he cannot conceive of it not raining as a goal or an end that he could pursue. It is not up to him whether it rains or not. Christine Collins, on the other hand, does have a goal: finding her son. This is an exceedingly difficult goal to achieve and all the indications are that it is unattainable. Nevertheless, she maintains her commitment to it and does what little she can to attain it. Hers is a paradigm example of what Shade understands hope to be.

Shade was not the first philosopher to see hope as closely connected to action. As we saw in the Introduction, Aquinas defined hope as the desire to act in pursuit of a future good that is arduous and difficult – but nevertheless possible – to obtain. If what is hoped for is conceived as the goal of an action that differs from others goals of action in that it is arduous and difficult but possible to obtain then there seems to be an inextricable link between hope and action. While this conception of hope is different from the one I have been developing, it seems to have some plausibility. It seems intuitively clear that whenever we act we hope for the outcome our action pursues. If I am walking to the university, then it could be said that I hope to get there. If I am putting on my socks, then it could be said that I hope to be wearing my socks. The reason these examples do not sound immediately apt is that these are actions the goals of which are very easy to achieve. I set about the task and I achieve it as a matter of course. I do not have to overcome any obstructions. While it is obvious that I intend to get to university or to put on my socks, respectively, I would not normally describe myself as hoping to achieve these things. This is because there is no difficulty in achieving them. There seems to be no gap, no uncertainty or no hindrance between forming the intention to do such things and actually doing them and achieving the intended outcome. The element of arduousness or difficulty that Aquinas points to is absent. On the other hand, if I take on something difficult – lifting a heavy load in the gymnasium, for example – I might indeed be self-consciously hoping that I achieve the goal. I form the intention but my agency does not just flow through to the action to put that intention immediately into effect. My action does not flow through smoothly to the attainment of my goal. There is a difficulty that I am aware of and I respond to that difficulty by hoping that I succeed. I should also respond to that difficulty by making an effort to succeed. If there are steps I could take to make success more likely – by using the correct lifting techniques, for example – then I should take them. But I am aware that the task is a challenging one and that my efforts may not be adequate to the task. Accordingly, I do not only intend to lift the weight or make the strenuous effort; I also find myself hoping that I will succeed.

Shade and Aquinas have captured an important point: that hope accompanies action, especially in cases where there is some difficulty in achieving what one intends to achieve. There are many examples where intending to do something and beginning to do it do not guarantee success. One must make an effort or be persistent. One must continue on despite setbacks. One must face dangers or difficulties with courage or determination. One must be resourceful or strategic. In all such cases one will do more than just intend to achieve the outcome and set about the task. One will also hope to succeed. Hope will be necessary here as a motivator for the effort required to attain the goal.

But there is a sense in which this applies to all actions, even ones that are not difficult. Even when I am putting on my socks it is possible – although extremely unlikely – that I will hurt my back in such a way that I am not able to bend down enough to complete the task. Even when I am walking to university it is possible – although very unlikely – that I will be hit by a car and prevented from completing my journey. Although these mishaps are unlikely, they are possible, and that possibility introduces an element of uncertainty or even risk into my life as an agent. Every action that I set out to perform is accompanied by an element of anxiety – however small – as to whether I shall be able to achieve what I set out to achieve. This anxiety may be vanishingly mild in the case of putting on my socks, but it will be more present to me in the case of lifting the weight. In more complex actions or courses of action, such as working towards a university degree or bringing up my children, this anxiety will be an ever-present element of doubt, concern and uncertainty that will both enliven and darken my involvement in those courses of action. I can never be sure of success. There is a multitude of circumstances or events that could frustrate my efforts and undermine my achievements. In the face of all this I will need determination, courage, commitment and endurance. What will motivate these stances if not hope for success?

When discussing the psychological states that accompany action most philosophers concentrate on the intentions that lead us to act. According to their account, every deliberate action is directed, as it were, by an intention that I have. I might not always be conscious of this intention, but if I were asked why I am putting on my socks, for example, I would have an answer. My actions have goals which I can bring to mind if I need to. It is this which defines these events as actions, as opposed to reactions or reflex movements. If what I am doing is performing an action then, by definition, I am pursuing a goal, and I have the intention of attaining that goal. In this way intentions are inextricable from actions. However, my suggestion is that there is at least one more element involved: hope. I not only intend to achieve my goal but I also hope to. This hope will be more present to my self-awareness when the action or course of action is difficult or risky, but I would suggest that it is present in a non-explicit way even in simple actions that are easy to perform. Between the intention and the successful completion of the action there is always room for bad luck to intervene. I may put my back out reaching down to put on my socks. I may have my studies interrupted by a death in my family. My children may suffer illness. There is always a gap between our intentions and the achievement of what we intend, which our efforts may not overcome. There is always the possibility of failure. Our intentions cannot bridge this gap. We do not have complete control over our circumstances. Accordingly, our hoping bridges the gap. This will be clear and apparent in cases where the gap looms large – as when the task is arduous and difficult – but it is also the case even when the action is easy and routine. Fate can always intervene and frustrate our intentions. Deep down we know this and, accordingly, deep down we supplement our intentions with hope.

As Aquinas suggests, when we set out on an arduous or difficult course of action, we hope to achieve our goal. This hope accompanies our intention and our agency. In so far as we cannot be sure of success, we hope for it. My suggestion is that, at an implicit and deep level of our consciousness, this structure of hope accompanies all our actions because of our implicit and deep awareness of our vulnerability to bad luck and mishap. Hope is our existential response to the contingency that is a mark of all our actions and of the world we live in.

Of course we can also respond to this contingency by taking care when we act, by making the required effort and by planning. Planning is often required in a course of action. By ensuring that we have prepared for our action by, for example, acquiring the right tools, engaging in the right training, or dividing up the task into its constituent parts we can be more assured of success. In this way planning is an important preparation for action and, in so far as it gives us some assurance of success, lessens the need for hope. Indeed, it is interesting to note that planning is similar to hope in that it is directed towards the future and what is possible but contingent. Moreover, it is motivated by a desire for success and, sometimes, by anxiety about failure. Yet it differs from hope in that it is an attempt to control the circumstances of one's action and the means at one's disposal so as to ensure a successful outcome, while hope becomes relevant when we recognize that our control has limits. It is when we see that, despite our planning and preparation, success is not certain that we find ourselves hoping for it. John's situation is an extreme example of this. In his case, there is nothing he can do to control the weather. Accordingly, the only psychological state that is available to him when he does not want to get wet is to hope that it does not rain.

So far we have been discussing how hope contributes to our agency: how it accompanies our actions because we intuitively know that our efforts may not be effective enough to realize our intentions and goals. But there is also another question that has arisen for us in the example of Christine Collins: is it necessary for hope to be expressed in action? Is hope that does not lead to action somehow incomplete and, as such, not a genuine case of hope?

Perhaps we should consider a further example here. Tony is a young man studying at the university who describes himself as hoping to go to South America to teach English there after he graduates. But at this present time he is doing nothing to realize this hope. He is studying, certainly, and this can contribute to the attainment of what he hopes for, but he has formed no specific plan to go to South America at any specific time and his course of study is not directly or deliberately designed to give him the qualifications needed to teach English in a Spanish-speaking country. In the absence of a purposeful course of action designed to realize his hope, we might be tempted to say that he merely wishes to go to South America: that he is engaged in wishful thinking. If he genuinely hopes to go, we would expect to see – if not now, then in the near future – some activity on his part designed to realize that goal. Can Tony hope for that goal without also intending to achieve it and acting to bring it about? Is hope a psychological state that is distinct from action or are we inclined to say that if Tony hopes for something that he could achieve by setting out on a course of action to achieve it, then his hope is empty or inauthentic if he does not set out on that course of action? We would not say that he hoped to go to South America if he were just waiting for a chance event to occur, such as winning the lottery so that he could pay the costs of going. Perhaps it is enough if he thinks that, at some future time, he will set about doing what he needs to do in order to travel to South America. For the moment he is concentrating on his studies and not forming any plans. But he has a vague and non-specific intention to do something about it in due course. And this vague idea that he has about his future could be described as his hoping that he will go. He is not unaware that he will need to do something about it at some time, but he does not feel ready to do so yet. For the moment he only hopes that he will go to South America.

The concept of hope has a slightly different meaning here. In this context, it is not the case that Tony hopes for an outcome because he knows that his efforts to attain that outcome are vulnerable to failure. Rather, he hopes for the outcome because he is not yet ready to embark on that project. At this stage going to South America is only a hope. It is not yet a plan or a project and it is not yet a specific intention. Indeed, it is probably fair to say that it is not very different from a wish and it may be that he has used the word in a misleading way when he described himself as hoping that he would go to South America. We could say that he wants to go to South America or that he wishes to but, in so far as he is not yet ready to take any action in order to achieve what he wants, we might not describe him as hoping that he will go. On the other hand, perhaps what he is hoping for is that circumstances will arise that will allow him to go. Some of these circumstances might be achievements of his, such as obtaining his university degree, while others will be due to others or to luck, such as his aunt giving him the money to go or his winning the lottery. The last two will be circumstances that are necessary for his going but are not under his control. Tony can only hope that, like the weather in John's case, these circumstances will come about. There are some things he can do to attain his goal, and he ought to set about doing them, but there are other circumstances that he can only hope will come about because they are not up to him.

These reflections lead me to disagree with Shade and Aquinas. For them, hopes, goals and actions are inextricably linked. Hope without action would be inauthentic. While there is some truth in this, I have argued that hope arises at precisely the point where agency leaves off. We entertain hope in respect of those conditions that are necessary for our achieving our goals but which we cannot bring about ourselves. Hope covers the gap between effort and outcome and where that gap is extremely small no hope is needed, while where it is huge hope is all we have. So in a case where we embark on an action that is simple to perform and of which the outcome is easily achieved, we have no need to hope that we will achieve that outcome, while in John's case, where there is nothing that he can do to achieve what he wants – that it will not rain – all he can do is hope for that eventuality.

Hoping and praying

In cases where there is nothing we can do to achieve our goal, our hoping may well be an appeal to powers other than our own. We often hear people say, especially in cases such as that of Fatima or Christine Collins, that they "hope and pray" that their child will be found. Perhaps in such cases the words "hope" and "pray" are linked simply to heighten the rhetorical effect and convey the urgency of the situation. At other times the word "prayer" seems to be a synonym for "hope", as when we say that the hapless goal-kicker who has no hope of kicking the goal "doesn't have a prayer". And yet hoping and praying do seem to be two different psychological states. John would have to be an ardent believer in an interventionist God if he prayed that it would not rain. But suppose he did. In what might the difference between such a prayer and a hope consist?

The nature of prayer is a deep and complex theological issue. It has to do with a person's relationship with their god and the forms that their communication with that god might take. It involves attitudes of adoration and worship, of reverence and gratitude, and of contemplation and meditation. It takes a person out of the humdrum existence of daily life and into a transcendent realm of ultimate realities. But the aspect that I am interested in here is that of supplication. Even if many theologians argue that God does not intervene in human affairs in any direct and specific way and does not respond to human intercessions, most religious believers address their gods in order to petition them for favours or for help with the problems of life. Some people pray for rain or for boun-teous harvests, while others pray for help in times of trouble. Even if such people also accept their god's will, manifested through what actually happens, as definitive of what *should* happen, they will pray for the outcome they hope for. We could imagine that if Christine Collins were religious in this way, she would pray that her child be found. How would such a prayer differ from her hope that her child be found?

However much you accept the finality of God's will, to pray is to suppose that you do have some control over the outcome in that you can invoke higher powers to assist you. While you may not be able to secure the desired outcome yourself, your god may come to your aid and secure it for you. This is both an acknowledgement of the limitations of your own powers and an attempt to overcome them. This suggests that prayer is a religious form of hope. It may be tempered by the humble realization that your god has better things to worry about than your puny problems, but it is nevertheless an attempt to invoke the divine powers and bring them into alignment with your hopes. For a non-religious person this will seem like wishful thinking, but for a religious believer it expresses a belief in a correspondence between the will of their gods and the wishes of mere mortals. If such an alignment is believed in strongly, it would turn hope into faith. That is a matter we shall explore later. For the moment I want to argue that the differences between hoping and praying are very subtle.

In the form of supplication, prayers are communications directed towards a higher power. Even in the form of worship or contemplation, they are understood as forms of communion with such powers. Prayers address a divine being. This is a clear and obvious difference between prayers and hopes. Hopes are directed upon positive outcomes, while prayers are addressed to a being who the supplicant imagines can bring the positive outcome about. Sometimes this may be an implicit address in which the person praying does not explicitly address herself to her god but feels a more inchoate wish for that outcome and an unspoken surrender to what will be. And yet, in so far as this is expressive of desire and anxiety as well as of a recognition of the limitation of her own powers to bring the positive outcome about, it is very similar to hope. In hope one is appealing to fate rather than a god and hoping that fate will deliver the desired outcome. It may be that in a subtle way John's hope that it does not rain is an appeal that he sends out to the cosmos that the forces of nature will not produce rain. As the French existentialist philosopher Gabriel Marcel (1889–1973) has put it, "Hope consists in asserting that there is at the heart of being, beyond all data, beyond all inventories and all calculations, a mysterious principle which is in connivance with me" (1995: 28). In hope one asks the cosmic powers to take one's interests to heart. One places one's trust in something that will respond to one's anxieties. One appeals to the beneficence of a superhuman power. In hope, one recognizes the limitations of what one can achieve by oneself and so makes an appeal to something beyond oneself. As with prayer, hope involves humility in admitting the limitations of one's control over the situation. Because one knows that bad luck can always intervene or that nothing that one could do will ensure that the desired outcome comes about, one throws oneself on the mercy of fate and appeals to vaguely understood cosmic powers to produce it. If this is right then the element of supplication that is definitive of prayer is present even in hope. The Catholic philosopher Peter Geach has argued that any rational hope must be grounded in Christian hope, saying that if "there is not this hope, then all hope is in vain" (1977: 48). As Christian hope is directed towards God, this claim makes the element of supplication in hope very explicit.

Not everyone will agree that hope involves supplication because it does not accord with the way that they feel when they hope. People with no religious faith, especially, will not be inclined to think that they are appealing to supernatural powers when they hope. I would not deny this. However, I would suggest that the structure of one's attitudes is similar when one prays and when one hopes. When one prays for help one is appealing to supernatural powers such as spirits, saints or a god by addressing them in supplication. The structure of this frame of mind includes an implicit acknowledgement of one's need for assistance and an explicit address to those powers that can provide it. One feels humble and powerless in comparison to the cosmos and one addresses the gods in pursuit of help. The structure of one's attitude includes a feeling of relative powerlessness and a space into which one inserts the saint, angel, god or supernatural agency that one can address and appeal to. When one hopes one does not make such an address and one does not explicitly appeal to supernatural forces. But there is still this space that one would like to fill with a power that will accord help – into which one would like to insert Marcel's "mysterious principle which is in connivance with me". Even without a god to appeal to, one's sense of relative powerlessness still obtains. Consequently, the inclination to make an unspoken appeal to forces greater than oneself is still latently present. Because an element of supplication is present in both, hoping and praying are not as different as secular thinkers would like to believe.

In many cases, however, the object of this supplication will not be a supernatural agency, however vaguely conceived, but another person or group of persons. Very often when we hope for something we send out an implicit or explicit appeal to someone else to help us achieve what we hope for. Or we might hope that our community or our government will help us achieve what we hope for. Even when such appeals are not explicit they can be present in the very psychological make-up of our hopes. The person or community that we appeal to will be specified by the nature of the hope that we are entertaining. Sometimes our supplication is directed at clinicians, sometimes at family members, and sometimes at politicians or community leaders. We may even address it in a playful way to imaginary figures such as Santa Claus. We shall explore these ideas further in later chapters.

The ethics of hope

If we summarize what we have discovered thus far we will see that there are elements of ethical significance in hope. I have suggested that hopes are a subcategory of wishes for outcomes judged to be good, which differ from other wishes in that they are motivated by a degree of anxiety or concern about specific circumstances in the world and in that they are limited to what the person who hopes considers both possible and contingent. Oriented to an uncertain future that we cannot completely control, our hopes express our acknowledgement that whatever happens is limited by our finite and fallible capacities and by the laws of physics. There may be a prayer-like element of supplication in our hope but the risk that what we hope for might not happen is something we have to live with. That we have to live within such limitations is what makes hope a virtue. To live within our limitations is of ethical value in that it is conducive to living life happily.

Moreover, there are further ethical or normative elements in hope. It is a wish that differs from other wishes in that it should motivate us to appropriate action when that is possible. While wishes can stay in the realm of fantasy or daydream, hopes should lead us to take whatever action is available in order to pursue what we hope for. Taken together, the characteristics of hope that distinguish it from wishing show that hope involves an engagement with reality that wishing lacks. This engagement takes the form not only of being committed to any relevant actions that are available, but also of understanding what possibilities there are in the world for actions that would help us to realize our goals and what the likelihood is that we shall be able to do so. Unlike hoping, wishful thinking does not need to have regard for how the world is or for what is likely to occur in it. Hope needs to combine our desires, emotions, feelings and anxieties with beliefs about, and understandings of, the world. There is a cognitive dimension to hope that makes this psychological state amenable to rational appraisal. To hope for something requires that we make some assessment as to whether what we hope for is possible, likely or inevitable. We need to have an understanding of the world, of our place in it and of our social relationships. We need to understand and respect the laws of nature that science has disclosed to us. Accordingly, it is an ethical requirement that when we hope we ought to be realistic. If we are not realistic, we are likely to slip into wishful thinking.

Hope and reason

While there is probably some cognitive aspect to most emotions, this point shows that hope is not an emotion in any simple or purely reactive manner. It involves a relatively high degree of understanding of the world intermingled with the concerns and desires that we have. If placing hope into the broader category of wishes suggested that it was an emotion, we should now modify that suggestion by adding that it also involves knowledge, belief and understanding. This, in turn, suggests that the distinction philosophers are fond of making between cognitive states such as belief and knowledge on the one hand, and emotional or motivational states such as desires and wishes on the other, is not as sharp as traditional thinking would suggest.

The reason that this distinction was made at all was that it allowed us to understand the internal struggles we often find ourselves with and to articulate the ethical problems we face in daily life. We often find ourselves not doing what we think we ought to do. We often find ourselves succumbing to temptations or shying away from our obligations. One way of understanding this is to suppose that, inside us, there is a struggle between reason and responsible thought on the one hand and unruly emotions and desires on the other. The paradigm case of an emotion in this model is anger. Anger seems to come over us like a turbulent storm and it causes us to lose our self-control and our ability to think clearly or act responsibly. Desire, too, can overwhelm us in this way. Accordingly, ancient thinkers such as Plato (c.428–c.348 BCE), Christian moral theologians and modern philosophers such as Kant have taught that we should seek to control our emotions and allow reason to rule our lives. The emotions were not to be trusted, while reason was infallible if used correctly and without interference from the unruly passions. Reason was to be the motivator of our actions, while emotional reactions were to be controlled or suppressed. The distinction between reason and cognitive states on one side, and emotions and desires on the other side, ties in with this moralistic conception of human existence. Accordingly, it is of considerable interest to note that hope straddles the distinction. It is both cognitive and motivational, rational and emotional, active and reactive.

This being the case, it is appropriate to ask whether hoping can be rational. If it were purely emotional or reactive and if the distinction between reason and emotion were a sharp one, then it would not be. But if it has a cognitive dimension it can be. We can explore whether it is appropriate for a person to hope for something by asking whether the understanding of the world and what is possible or likely in it that is implicit in the hope is correct or rationally justifiable. Accordingly, hope as a virtue has a further normative feature. We have already seen that it should lead to appropriate action when such actions are available. We can now add that it should be rational rather than naive.

However, some argue that hopes do not need to be rational: that it is valid to "hope against hope". The Christine Collins example shows that hope can be valid as an emotional anchor: something that we cling to regardless of circumstances, regardless of what our reason tells us is happening or going to happen, and regardless of whether our hope is rational or irrational. Christine is hoping for something that she knows is extremely unlikely: finding her lost son after many years. And yet it may not be irrational to want such an outcome and thus to hope for it, no matter how unlikely it is. The finding of the other missing boy, David, has shown Christine that it is possible that her Walter is still alive. In this way her finding him still seems possible, however unlikely it is, and her psychological state can be, by our definition, one of hope. But if the hope is unrealistic or misguided, the actions it inspires will be futile or even damaging. Christine shows a kind of sad nobility in never giving up, but after a certain amount of time – five, ten, or twenty years – that sort of active pursuit would cease to be rational. One could imagine a family being torn apart through not accepting that the search has at some point become futile: so much potential going into pointless actions, perhaps siblings living in the missing child's shadow.

Sometimes, against all odds, the seemingly impossible happens, and the hope may turn out to be justified. But that is not an argument for the *rationality* of the hope.

So far we have agreed that it would be irrational to hope for something impossible since to do so would not be to hope but to engage in wishful thinking. On this view the less possible something is, the less rational it is to hope for it. But this does not seem to tell the whole story. Perhaps a rational assessment of possibility should not be the only criterion. After all, on those grounds it would seem irrational to hope for world peace or global justice. Christine Collins, whose child seems irrevocably lost but who goes on hoping, seems admirable even if not rational.

Perhaps the question of whether it is rational or irrational does not apply to the hope itself, but to the actions that hope inspires. Whether it is rational or irrational to hope that the child will be found, it will certainly be irrational to leave a place at the table for him each evening. In relation to Bob's lottery ticket, his hope that he wins is fairly irrational given the odds, but to spend the money he has not yet won would be an even more irrational action based on an irrational assessment of his chance of winning. On this view, although you cannot have an irrational hope, you can have an irrational assessment of your chances, and take irrational actions in response to the resulting expectations.

Nevertheless, to think of hope as a phenomenon that is outside the boundaries of rationality and as based on something distinct from rationality would be very problematic. On such a view, hope would be a specific form of wish while reasoning about the likelihood of the hoped-for outcome or about appropriate courses of action is a separate matter. On this view hope would be nothing more than an emotional anchor that can give us a break from our reason and rationality. I shall argue in later chapters that this view contains many dangers.

Hope as a virtue

We saw in the Introduction that Aristotle gives us a structure for thinking about virtues that might help us to understand hope further. We have just been exploring the cognitive and rational aspects of hope, which are relevant to seeing it as what Aristotle called an "intellectual virtue". But in the Introduction we also saw the way in which Aristotle understood the virtues that relate to our desires and emotions as states of mind that could be understood as occupying an appropriately moderate position between two relevant extremes. Given that hope also relates to our desires, emotions and anxieties, can this model be used to further explicate hope as a virtue? I would suggest that it can. Although I suggested that hope is not itself felt in differing degrees, it can make sense to describe it as being more or less intense depending on the other psychological states that contribute to it. Accordingly, hope can be situated in the middle of a spectrum of psychological states, at one end of which are states of excess and at the other end of which are states of deficiency. On this model, I would suggest that the extremes that virtuous hope avoids are presumption, resignation and despair.

Presumption is an excess of hope. It consists in being overconfident that the good outcome for which one hopes will come about. Presumption lacks the sense of uncertainty that is a defining characteristic of hope. This may lead the presumptuous person to make inadequate efforts in securing the desired good outcome on the grounds that he believes that things will turn out well whether or not he makes such efforts. Moreover, we can understand presumption as an excessive expression of the element of supplication that is inherent in hope. The presumptuous person is one who feels overly confident that whatever cosmic powers are out there are indeed on his side and are indeed in connivance with him, as Marcel had put it. Accordingly, those powers can be relied on to ensure that the desired outcome will occur. Indeed, an even more extreme form of such presumption is the feeling that one is entitled to the good outcome or deserves it in some way, either because one has been good or because one has placed trust in those powers or gods. Authentic hope would never go so far.

At the other end of the spectrum is despair: a deficiency of hope. Despair consists in not being able to hope because one has lost all confidence that things could turn out well. Not only does one feel certain that things will turn out for the worst, but, even more deeply, one is unable to commit to any judgement that a future state might be good for one. Nothing seems worth doing and no prospects of success seem to be on offer. Despair is the absence of hope. But if despair is the most deficient state in the spectrum of variations of hope, there is another state that could be identified on the deficient side of that spectrum, although it does not stand at its extreme end. This state is resignation. Resignation is an attitude that accepts that the desired good outcome that one had hoped for will not come about. It is an acceptance that things are not going to go one's way. One begins to think that the outcome is not possible and so hope fades. One no longer approaches the relevant circumstances in one's life with expectation and one no longer seeks – whether through supplication directed at others or through one's own efforts – the goods that one had hoped for. Accordingly, one gives up making an effort and the scope of one's world contracts a little. Life has less to offer and hope lies defeated.

As we move from the excess of presumption, through appropriate hope, and on to resignation and despair, we may suppose that the final state would be depression. However, I think of depression more as a psychological pathology than as an attitude that could be appraised in ethical terms. Depression is not a vice, but an illness.

Conclusion

We can now add to what we learnt from the earlier example of John and summarize our exploration of the differences between hopes and wishes so as to offer a definition of hope. A hope is a wish that differs from other wishes in that:

- it is motivated by felt needs or some degree of anxiety or concern, as opposed to fantasy or wishful thinking;
- it implies a judgement that what is hoped for is something good;
- its object is an occurrence that is considered to be possible;
- its object is an occurrence that is considered to be not inevitable;
- it is directed towards the future as conceived by the person who hopes;
- the person hoping is uncertain as to whether what is hoped for will happen;
- it is directed to circumstances over which the person hoping does not have complete control;
- it ought to lead to appropriate action on the part of the person who hopes when such action is available;
- it has the psychological structure of supplication; and
- it ought to be rational and realistic.

Even though I have called these defining features of hope, it must not be thought that I am being prescriptive about how the word "hope" should be used in ordinary English. I am not legislating that if someone says that they hope that it does not rain when they are firmly convinced that it will, or that if they say that they hope for a good outcome but are not prepared to do anything to secure it, they are misusing the word and that they should have said that they are entertaining a wish. People will understand their meaning either way. However, I am suggesting that for a hope to be rational, admirable or genuine – for it to play the existential role in our lives of grounding our commitments and courses of action – it should fulfil these ten conditions. Any expressed hope that does not do so is an inauthentic hope. If hope is to be regarded as a virtue, then we must have reason to admire it and to regard it as a positive character trait. As a virtue it stands in an appropriate median position between the extremes of presumption and despair. The ten conditions I have identified give us ways of understanding and evaluating how hope might be admirable as a virtue.

2. Being hopeful

So far we have been considering examples in which the hope being discussed is more or less episodic. What I mean by this is that there was a definite and relatively short period during which the hope was entertained. John hoped that it would not rain on the day that he needed to go to university and was at risk of getting wet. When the circumstances change, the hope is no longer apposite and so disappears. My hope that I receive a CD for Christmas will cease – either with satisfaction or disappointment – at Christmas. Fatima hoped that her child would be found for as long as it was not found. However, Christine Collins's hope continued indefinitely and raised the difficult questions we have noted about how such hopes are related to action and whether such hopes could be rational. It will be interesting to explore why such cases of temporally open-ended hopes raise such difficult questions.

One way of approaching this issue is by noting a technical feature of hopes. Hopes are directed upon objects. One hopes that some event will occur, that one will obtain some item or that one attains some goal. John hopes that it will not rain; I hope to receive a Miles Davis CD; Bob hopes to become rich; Fatima hopes that her child is found; Tony hopes to go to South America. These are all hopes *for* something. In technical philosophical terms we describe this by saying that hopes are "intentional" psychological states. This usage of the word differs from that usage where we describe actions as "intentional" when they are engaged in to achieve a goal. Our more technical usage derives from the Latin words "*in*", meaning "in", and "*teneo*", meaning "to hold". It means that one holds something in one's thoughts or that one has an object in mind. To say that hoping is an intentional state is to say that it is directed upon an "object" in this technical sense. More specifically one hopes to attain that object, whether it be its not raining, the present of a CD, becoming rich, the finding of a child, or having the opportunity to travel to South America. Accordingly, a hope lasts only as long as the object is not attained. When John completes his journey without its having rained, when I receive the CD I had hoped for, when Bob wins the lottery, when Fatima has her child returned to her, and when Tony flies off to Rio, the hopes in question cease to exist. In this way the temporality of hopes is tied to the intentionality of hopes.

What makes this rather technical point interesting is that there are also relevant psychological states that are not intentional and therefore not so temporally constrained. We sometimes speak of a person as being optimistic or as having a hopeful outlook on life. Let us call this person Lynne. Lynne has a sunny disposition, always sees the good in people and constantly believes that things will turn out for the best. While she may hope for this or that specific outcome from time to time, the most notable feature of her personality is that she is hopeful in a general way. This hopefulness is not a specific hope for a concrete outcome, but a general mood that she has or a general attitude that she displays towards the world and her life in it. In this way, her hopefulness is not intentional. It is not directed upon a specific object or outcome. It is rather like wearing rose-coloured glasses, which lead her to see the whole world in a rosy manner. Of course, her experiences of the world are intentional in the sense that they are experiences of specific objects and things in the world. But the rosiness of her experience is not the object of her experience. It is the *way* in which she experiences those objects. She does not see her rose-coloured glasses. She sees the world *through* those glasses. She always sees the good side of people and always believes that things will turn out well.

The anxieties she feels and the things she worries about are met with confidence and a preparedness to take the necessary risks. Her hopefulness is not constituted as a set of hopes directed upon specific outcomes, but is a way in which she apprehends the whole world and everything that happens in it. For her, hopefulness is a way of being.

But if Lynne's hopefulness is a way of being in this way and is not evoked by being directed upon specific objects, then it is not subject to the temporal constraints that hopes are. Whereas a hope only lasts as long as the period during which the relevant situation that is the object and context of the hope is not resolved, hopefulness has no such temporal limits. It passes from one situation to the next indefinitely and continues to colour the world in which Lynne lives. Hopefulness is not an intentional psychological state and, as a result, it is not temporally constrained. It can last a lifetime. Of course, if Lynne were to suffer constant disappointments and rebuffs, her disposition might change and she may cease being a hopeful person, but this will be a gradual change and one that affects the whole of her personality.

It is clear that hope and hopefulness are concepts that are closely related. But hope is more episodic. This becomes clearer when we consider the word as a verb rather than a noun. There are specific times or periods of time during which a person hopes for something. In contrast, hopefulness is a character trait that marks a person's way of being for significant lengths of time, if not their whole life. Again, to hope for something is to direct one's attention to that something in particular, but to be hopeful is to be inclined to see everything in optimistic terms.

Hopefulness can be understood not only as a character trait, but also as a quality of experience. If Lynne sees the world through rose-coloured glasses, then her experience of the world is qualitatively different from that of a person who has a less optimistic view. Hopefulness makes every moment in life a new beginning. If every situation is seen through hopefulness then it contains a promise of something new and exciting. That most hopeful of philosophers Friedrich Nietzsche (1844–1900) said that the noble and free-spirited person knows how to forget. Rather than carry the slights, disappointments and resentments of the past into the future, such a person enters every situation with the hope of a new beginning and a new birth of possibilities. This disposition could not arise from what one has learnt in a troublesome and vicious world: it arises from the mysterious depths of one's being. One is hopeful for the future despite the past rather than because of it. It is the person who can look forward to new and exciting things in the future despite having suffered disappointments and hardships in the past who is truly hopeful. Such a person is less inclined to let fears about the future or resentments about the past influence their present dispositions. It would take the science of psychology to explain why some people are more hopeful than others. For philosophy it is enough to observe that hopefulness is the fragile strength of personality that inclines Lynne to embrace the world and her life in it with such a positive outlook.

This is especially relevant when we consider interpersonal relationships. Whenever Lynne meets a new person she is generous and warm towards them. If there is anything untrustworthy about them, she gives them the benefit of the doubt. If they are well disposed towards her, her warmth will lead them to be even better. Her hopefulness is an encouragement to them and she herself gains from the greater depth and trust that exists between them. The future orientation of hope means that every friend and acquaintance holds the promise of shared enrichment and enjoyment. When she comes home from work and greets her partner the joy she feels at seeing him, and which she spreads to him with her greeting, is enlivened with a hopefulness that they can both feel and which augurs well for an intimate evening of rapport and companionship.

Hopefulness is an essential ingredient in joyfulness. To live life with joy is to be able to project the promise of a hopeful future for oneself and for others. Life is full of surprises. The hopeful person sees this as a source of joy while the pessimist sees it as a threat. The pessimist fears the new and the strange, while the hopeful person accepts and delights in it. In this way, hopefulness becomes a constituent of courage, trust and tolerance as well as of joy and love.

These points about hopefulness as a way of being and of seeing the world allow me to return to the observations I made about the cognitive dimension of hope. In the preceding chapter I argued that hope involves beliefs and cognitive judgements that ought to be realistic and rational. Yet, my classifying it as a specific form of wish tended to stress the emotional and desirous side of hope. If this had led me to ignore the cognitive aspects of hope I would have become trapped in the philosophers' distinction between beliefs and desires, reason and emotion, and cognitive and motivational psychological states. The concept of hopefulness allows us to understand further how hope is a state that straddles these distinctions. Hope is a cognitive stance marked by the emotional quality of hopefulness, while hopefulness is a future-oriented way of seeing and understanding the world that is trusting, confident and optimistic.

I should not create the impression that hopefulness and optimism are the same. They are clearly related and have similar features, but there is a crucial difference between them. The optimistic person is one who believes that everything will turn out well. Optimism is predominantly a cognitive state. It is a framework of belief through which the world is seen as orderly, controllable, prone to good outcomes and free of dire risks. The optimist believes that things will turn out well and that her projects will succeed. The hopeful person, on the other hand, has a more practical orientation. Her hopefulness is constituted by a willingness to act in pursuit of her goals, to accept the risks, to make the required efforts and to accept the outcomes even if they are disappointing. It is a practical stance rather than a cognitive belief. Patrick Shade defines hopefulness as "an attitude of energetic openness and readiness to promising possibilities" (2001: 135), although he recognizes that this attitude is vulnerable to life's disappointments. This describes an action-oriented character trait in which a person is prepared to see difficulties and obstructions as challenges to be overcome rather than as risks to be avoided. Hopefulness is the willingness to grasp the nettle and act in the pursuit of one's goals in the face of the hurdles that need to be overcome or risks that need to be borne. In this respect it is more akin to confidence or courage than it is to optimism. But, just like hope, courage and confidence, it needs to be realistic and rational.

Subjectivity

Now that we have begun talking about character traits rather than episodic psychological states such as hopes and desires, we need to delve more deeply into the categories we use to describe our inner lives. If we were psychologists trying to understand character traits, we would speak of dispositions, which are manifested in what people say or do. Dispositions and the actions that they lead to are the outward manifestations of peoples' inner states. However, as philosophers we ought to try to understand these inner states in their own terms by reflecting on how we experience them. Reflection on our experiences and on the way we react to the world and to other people reveals many hidden depths. We often don't fully understand why we do things and why we react to others and to challenges in the world in the way that we do. When it comes to such intense experiences as love, fear and joy we find ourselves experiencing depths that we can barely fathom. What goes on inside us – what I call our "subjectivity" – is mysterious to us. We know that it is difficult to understand other people and what makes them tick, but it is even more difficult to understand ourselves, even when reflection gives us a large amount of data. Sigmund Freud (1856–1939) was the most famous thinker of the recent past to make the point that we are often motivated or driven to action by inner forces that we neither understand nor easily accept. For Freud, our subjectivity is hidden, complex and perhaps even dangerous. Many novelists recognize this also and portray it powerfully in their stories.

The lesson I want to draw from these observations is that the distinction philosophers make between beliefs and desires, however useful it might be in mapping our various psychological states, is relatively superficial. Beliefs and desires are states of which we can be reflectively aware. They are states we can become aware of through introspection. This is especially true if they are intentional states. If I have a definite belief about something – that it is raining outside, for example – I will also be aware that I have that belief. If someone asks me whether it is raining, I will be able to answer them. If I have a desire for a slice of cheesecake, I will be aware that I have that desire, especially if I am confronted with such a slice. These are psychological states that lie close to the surface of my subjectivity, as it were, and of which I can be readily aware through reflection. But there are also deeper currents in my psychological make-up. There are fundamental drives, appetites, instincts, insecurities, convictions and commitments of which I might not be fully aware but that influence the way I live my life and motivate me to do the things that I do. But we should not think of this only in the negative terms that Freud suggests. We don't only do things that we might come to regret; we also draw on deep wells of creativity, determination and love, which drive us to positive actions that may surprise us. Who can understand the courage of the person who places himself at risk to save another? Who can really understand why they love the person they love? Almost any form of explanation will fail to capture the depth and wonder of such phenomena.

I would propose that hopefulness is a trait that belongs to this deeper stratum of human subjectivity. Intentional psychological states are directed towards objects and are thus available to self-awareness and reflection. But non-intentional psychological states are not so directed and are thus not readily available to self-awareness. These are states of which we are not easily conscious. Hope is an intentional state that lies near the surface of our subjectivity and can thus be readily brought to awareness, while hopefulness is a deeper structure of our subjectivity that is largely hidden from introspective view. Just as the rose-coloured glasses through which Lynne sees the world are not directly seen by her as an object of her vision, so what the hopeful person is aware of is not her hopefulness but rather the world seen as a place filled with positive possibilities. And if these deeper strata of our being are hidden from our consciousness, they will not be readily scrutinized for their rationality either.

Philosophers have speculated about what the deepest springs of our motivations are and have formulated theories about these hidden strata of our subjectivity for thousands of years. Aristotle, as we saw in the Introduction, argued that all human beings have an inherent tendency to pursue happiness and that this tendency is the hidden basis of all their reasons for action. If you asked John, for example, why he was going to the university, he might answer that it was to attend his class. If you asked why he was attending his class, he might answer that it was to obtain a high grade in his course of study. If you persisted and asked why he wanted that, he might answer that he needed to get a good job. If you continued asking why, he might say that he wanted to live comfortably and be able to support a family. Eventually, though, he would run out of answers and he would be pressed to say something vague such as that he pursued these goals in order to be happy. He might not know what this means exactly, but he would have reached a point where he has given an answer such that it is no longer rational to ask for a reason for pursuing that goal. The conversation would have reached a point where it can only be assumed that both John and his interviewer understand the answer because both share – at an implicit level – some understanding of what the ultimate goal of everyone's striving is. The point is not that they both have an articulate theory about what happiness is, but that they both recognize that once that answer has been given, it makes no further sense to ask why anyone would pursue that goal. In this way Aristotle argues that happiness is our ultimate goal in life. He then goes on to describe what it is that would make people happy. But his main point is that it is in the nature of human beings to seek happiness – whatever that turns out to be – and that all the specific and day-to-day goals that they pursue at particular times take their meaning and significance from being expressions of that fundamental quest.

It seems to me that it follows from this rather abstract point – abstract because it does not explicate what happiness consists in – that hopefulness is a fundamental structure of human existence. At a deep, constant and inarticulate level of our subjectivity we hope to be happy. This hope motivates all our intentional actions and provides the backdrop against which they can be seen as rationally chosen episodes in a human life. The quotations from Aquinas and Kant in the Introduction assume the same point, although they presuppose differing views on what happiness is.

Before exploring this matter further, I should waylay a possible objection. It might seem to follow from the idea that we all inherently pursue our happiness that we are all inherently selfish. On this view, whatever our surface intentions might be – whether to help a friend or to perform a socially valuable task – our more deep-seated motivation will always be to satisfy our longing for happiness. But my interpretation of Aristotle's idea does not imply this. It may well be that when we explore what happiness is, we find it can only be attained by looking after the needs of others, especially those whom we love, and by contributing to the lives of our communities. Our hopefulness in relation to happiness would then come to expression in acts of generosity and concern for those others and by living our lives within our community's norms. The notion of "selfishness" does not mean that we are motivated by our own deepest hopes and concerns. It means that we consciously pursue our own interests at the expense of the interests of others. There are very few philosophers who think that happiness can be attained in that way. Acting from love for, or caring about, others may very well be a path to happiness. The key point is that, even if my deep and hidden motivation for helping others is my hope for happiness, this does not negate the fact that my surface and conscious motivation is the desire to help those others. And the moral quality of my action arises from my conscious intention rather than from my hidden motivations. It is because my reason for action is to help others that it is an ethical and selfless act. That this leads to my being happy is a fortunate but unconscious and unintended by-product.

Indeed, there is a modern Aristotelian philosopher, the late Paul Ricoeur (1913–2005), who interprets Aristotle's claim that it is a basic tendency in all human beings to seek and hope for happiness by positing what he calls an "ethical aim" for all human beings. His suggestion is that what we all seek and hope for at a deep and inarticulate level of our being is "to live well, with and for others, in just institutions". What Ricoeur is doing here is filling out what happiness means in terms that are not centred just on the individual and his or her desires. The happiness we hope for does not consist just in our getting what we want. It also includes our having meaningful and loving relationships with others. Giving is just as constitutive of happiness as receiving. Our social lives and our lives of intimate rapport with those we love are just as much a part of our hope for happiness as are our pursuit of comfort and pleasure for ourselves. Moreover, Ricoeur is suggesting that our deepest hopefulness includes hopes for forms of social life that guarantee justice. We feel not only pity and anguish when we see other people suffer but also anger when we think their suffering is the result of exploitation, cheating, theft or any of the many other departures from the fair social and economic arrangements with which we seek to structure our lives. This is a very big thesis and much has been written to fill out the details, but the central point is that this ethical aim is an attempt to articulate what it is that we all hope for at a deep and inchoate level of our subjectivity.

I should add that to hope for something is, inevitably, also to fear the non-realization of our hope. Not only do we hope for happiness for ourselves, with others, and in a just society, but we also worry about our hopes being frustrated. When we love someone we not only wish good things for them but we also fear losing them or their suffering unhappiness. Our hopes have two sides: hopes for the good and fear of the bad. As Aquinas noted, the opposite of the good that we hope for is the bad that we fear. Accordingly, the deep and hidden levels of our subjectivity contain fears and concerns as well as hopes. Indeed, many of our hatreds stem from this level of our being. If we hope for justice we also hate injustice; if we love our communities we also hate those who would harm or attack those communities.

The problem of evil

This mention of fear and hatred reminds us that the world contains much evil. Human beings do terrible things to one another, ranging from theft, rape and murder to all-out war. Human beings seem driven by greed, lust and the quest for self-glorification to perpetrate crimes on an often horrific scale. Even if we do not actively commit such crimes, we may neglect the needs of millions who are starving or oppressed. The world is marked by suffering, starvation and injustice. If we were driven only by the hope for happiness and for social harmony and justice, how could things have gone so terribly wrong? Perhaps we are driven by deep and inchoate evil inclinations as well as good ones. Many hold the view, for example, that war cannot be eliminated from human history because human beings – and especially men – are inherently aggressive. While we should not ignore this possibility, one way of escaping the apparent logical link between evil in the world and evil inescapably present in the hearts of all human beings is to say that the evil that men do arises not from the intention to do evil, but from a misguided intention to do good.

Having suggested that our hope is to be happy, we need to say what happiness is. Having suggested that our ethical aim is to live well, with and for others, in just institutions, we need to say what living well is, which others we should live with and for, and what justice consists in. The unfortunate fact is that human beings have given different and conflicting answers to these questions over the ages. We live in a world marked by "values pluralism" in which the conceptions that people have of what it is to live a good life differ and come into conflict. If we form the view that we need to change, punish or even wipe out those people who disagree with us about such values, or about morality or religion, or who are of a different skin colour, or have a different sexual preference from us, then we may well end up doing what others regard as evil. But in our own hearts we will think that we are pursuing our ethical aim. What is needed to overcome this difficulty is rational discussion about what it is good to do in life and what forms of life are valid expressions of our hope for happiness or of our ethical aims. The history of philosophies, religions and political ideologies around the world is the history of such discussions, while the history of war, oppression and hatred is the history of their failure.

Another difficulty that might be raised is that the idea that we all entertain a fundamental hope for happiness in the deeper recesses of our subjectivity and that a minimal articulation of what such happiness might consist in – to live well, with and for others, in just institutions – is being offered without any factual evidence. Indeed, much of the evidence that might be cited actually counts against it. We have already noted that world history – a valid source of evidence on this question if ever there was one – does not seem to support the theory. There is too much evil in the world to bear it out. War, persecution, ethnic cleansing and terrorism seem to suggest that evil motivations occupy an equally fundamental place in our souls. It would seem that, while there is much good that takes place in the world, human history is at best equivocal on the question. But there is an even deeper problem. The fact is that no evidence that would settle the question of whether human beings are fundamentally good or evil is possible. I have said that we are talking about levels of our subjectivity that are not available to our reflection or scrutiny. How is it, then, that I can make claims about its content? Where could we find the evidence that we all have these fundamentally good motivations? If this deep level of our subjectivity is hidden and unarticulated, then what is the basis of my confidence that human beings are fundamentally good and hope for good things?

My answer is to say that I am not making a claim of the sort that requires factual or empirical evidence. I am not making a scientific, sociological, historical or psychological claim. To use a technical term, I am making a "hermeneutic" claim. What this means is that I am proposing a framework through which we *interpret* the human condition and human history rather than a thesis about fundamental and hidden human motivations that might be supported by empirical evidence. I am not saying that we should study human history and then conclude by some form of logical inference that human beings are good (or bad). Rather, I am suggesting that we might see human beings in this optimistic way because it is expressive of our own hopefulness about human beings. I am not making a factual claim, but asking us to see human beings in a hopeful way. Indeed, you might say that I am asking us to see human beings through rose-coloured glasses. If this is a rational way of seeing human beings it will be so, not because there is historical evidence for it, but because interpreting the human condition in this way is conducive to social solidarity and human happiness.

However, there is no denying that the evil that is caused by human beings – as opposed to the harm that comes from natural calamities – is a troublesome phenomenon. In the past and in many cultural traditions around the world, it was explained as being introduced into the world by a supernatural agency in the form of the devil or Satan. In the Christian tradition the devil is seen as a fallen angel created by God and allowed by him to engage in his evil ways upon this earth. Other cultural traditions also speak of evil spirits or agencies that wreak havoc in the world. It is part of this set of views that human beings are fundamentally weak and sinful and are vulnerable to the seductive overtures of such spirits. Indeed, Christianity teaches that original sin has tainted us and given us ineradicable inclinations to do evil. I have already mentioned the more secular philosophical view that we are divided internally between the good influences of reason and the bad influences of emotion and desire. Notice, by the way, that there is no scientific evidence for any of these views either. The only empirical evidence to which these views are a response is that human beings do things that others disapprove of and call evil. My point is this. Most accounts of human frailty, fallibility and fractiousness are invitations to see human events in a certain way; namely, through dark-coloured glasses rather than rose-coloured glasses. They urge us to adopt a negative hermeneutics of human reality rather than a positive one. The doctrine of original sin, for example, encourages us to see human beings as inherently evil and our deepest inclinations as morally problematic. But we are not forced by the evidence to take one view or another. We can choose the theory that best fits with our outlook and our hopes. Accordingly, it is a coherent explanation of the phenomenon of human-caused evil to suggest that while our fundamental drives are good, our understandings of how to pursue our fundamental hopes are often flawed. It is not that we are fundamentally evil or that we have fundamentally evil inclinations. Rather, we all want to live well, with and for others, in just institutions, but our ideas of what this amounts to or of what it requires of us in practical terms can lead us to do terrible things.

Nor does this deny that there may be some people whose upbringing has been such that they are motivated by anger, hatred, resentment or fear. Such people have little room in their lives for thinking about what they should do and often express themselves in ways that are harmful to others. My hopeful view does not seek to obscure such problems but it urges us to be generous-minded in our understanding of them.

Hopefulness as a virtue

In so far as hopefulness is conducive to living life well we can understand it as a virtue in Aristotle's non-moralistic sense of that term. Accordingly, how might Aristotle's analytical structuring of the virtues as situated between inappropriate extremes help us in understanding hopefulness?

Perhaps the extreme of too much hopefulness doesn't have a single word to describe it, but we can think of it as a form of naivety. If hopefulness is a tendency to see the world through rose-coloured glasses, then the glasses of a person who is naive in the relevant sense are too rosy. Such a form of naivety is a disposition to expect the best outcomes, see the best in others and remain positive despite disappointments. It is an excessive optimism and a naive confidence and trust in others. It is a deep inclination to evaluate risks too optimistically. The degree of hopefulness inherent in naivety is immune to any realistic appraisal of how the world is and how likely good outcomes are. It involves an irrational faith in the willingness of the gods to ensure that things will turn out well.

But in so far as we are describing a deep and inchoate stratum of our subjectivity that is largely hidden from self-reflection, we can posit a further form of excess of hopefulness, one that may have a deeper and causal relation to naivety. I am thinking of fantasy, understood as a kind of pre-intentional wishful thinking. We are all inclined to imagine ourselves as highly successful, or as happily cosseted in trouble-free relationships, or as rock stars, or as champion chefs. In this way, fantasy is a retreat from reality. But at a deeper and less articulate level, fantasy is not just thinking consciously about specific wonderful things that we would like to have happen to us. Rather, it is feeling so confident and powerful within ourselves that we take on any challenge and fail to look out for how things might go wrong. The deepest reaches of our being include inclinations to daydream and to embellish ourselves and our circumstances in ways that enhance the sense of our own capacities. This is a form of self-indulgence in which one imagines that one can do anything, be loved by everyone and right all wrongs. And this could motivate that form of wishful thinking that fails to take intelligent and measured action in the pursuit of what is wished for because it imagines itself capable of achieving it with ease. Fantasy comprises an excessive confidence in oneself. In short, whether in the form of naivety or fantasy, the excesses of hopefulness are pre-conscious dispositions that lead to the vice of presumption.

I further suggest that the extreme of too little hopefulness is cynicism. It might be thought that I would slot pessimism into Aristotle's structure here, but I don't think of pessimism as a pre-conscious emotional state or attitude. It is a belief about how things will turn out; namely, badly. It is a cognitive state that rates the probability of good outcomes as being very low. A pessimist thinks that success is too unlikely to be worth striving for and that our desires are too difficult to satisfy. But what we need in Aristotle's schema is a pre-intentional attitude or way of interpreting the world through our emotions and feelings. Cynicism is such a state. Its basic stance is that nothing is worth hoping for. Nothing is valuable enough to be bothered about. No goals have enough value for us to link our happiness to them. This is a lack of hopefulness because it refuses to give itself any objects of hope. For a cynic nothing matters. A cynic doesn't even strive to be happy.

Conclusion

Hopefulness, then, is a virtuous, deep structure of our subjectivity. It is a disposition through which we relate to life and to the world around us in a way that is conducive to our happiness. Our human subjectivity is defined and established by our hopefulness. Our deepest drive is to realize our hopes for happiness, for social existence and for justice. Although there can be no argument to show that such an attitude is empirically warranted, it can be justified by the warmth, generosity and courage with which it allows us to live our lives.

But there are two sides to this element in our deepest being. The deep structure of our subjectivity that I have identified as hopefulness has an obverse side: that of anxiety. If we hope for happiness, sociability and justice, we are also anxious about the possibility that these goals will be denied us. We are concerned for our happiness and worried that we may not attain it. We love others and worry that they will suffer hardship or disappointment. We are committed to social justice and are distressed when we see it so often denied. Hopefulness is not just a sunny disposition. It is the positive side of a host of deep concerns and anxieties. The hopeful person is the one who stresses the positive side while the less hopeful person is preoccupied with the anxieties. Hopefulness is an unarticulated but reasonable way of being in which we acknowledge the precariousness of our projects and the vulnerability of our existence and yet commit ourselves joyfully to the living of our lives.

This presence of anxiety in the deep subjectivity of the hopeful person indicates that the ten features of hope that I identified at the conclusion of the previous chapter apply to hopefulness also. The first of those features was that hope, and now hopefulness, are responses to anxieties either consciously entertained or inchoately felt in the very depths of our being. It is this duality in our existential make-up, along with the other features of hope and hopefulness on that list, that I shall explore and illustrate in the following chapters.

3. Hope in the clinic

By "hope in the clinic" I refer to a domain of life in which we deal with illness, injury and death. What role does hope play in this domain so that we can attain the kind of fulfilment that is specific to it? This is a question not only for those who suffer illness, injury or death and their families, but also for those who care for them, whether they be doctors, nurses, physiotherapists, psychiatrists or any of the many other healthcare professionals who look after people who are ill or dying. It has been established scientifically that patients with even the most dire injuries or serious medical conditions will enjoy better outcomes if they hope for such outcomes. There are said to be neuropsychiatric dimensions to hope and they can have therapeutic effects similar to pharmaceutical placebos. Hopeful patients live longer. Hope can lead not only to resilience in the face of suffering, but also to amelioration of the malady that is causing the suffering. In the field of palliative care, where patients are dying without any prospect of cure, hope is said to be an essential ingredient in the achievement of a "good death".

Moreover, healthcare workers themselves entertain hopes for their patients. But, whereas those hopes are informed by medical and therapeutic knowledge and are therefore likely to be realistic, the hopes of their patients and clients are motivated by anxieties about illness, injury and death and may therefore be inconsistent with realistic prognoses. Healthcare workers are taught that hope is a positive force that aids patients in their recovery and produces positive health outcomes, and they are enjoined not to take hope away from their patients. However, they are also enjoined not to give them "false hope". Nurses have been told that "a nurse inspires hope more by what she is than what she does" (Vaillot 1970: 272; quoted in Herth 2005: 175). Moreover, to put these admonitions on a more concrete and scientific footing, nursing and other health researchers have devised frameworks for observing hope in patients and scales for measuring it, and have developed techniques and interventions for maintaining and enhancing such hopes. This literature seems to suggest that hope is an entity that can be given to people or taken away from them and that can be measured and increased. Rather than pursue such scientific approaches, however, in this chapter I want to apply the analyses of hope and hopefulness developed in the previous two chapters to the clinical setting and to offer some reflections on ethical implications that arise in this setting. If it can make sense to say that a clinician can give a patient hope, it will be because that clinician has addressed one or more of the ten features of hope developed in Chapter 1: for example, by showing a patient new possibilities, reducing their uncertainty or responding to their supplication.

Illness and death

If hope and hopefulness are our positive reactions to anxieties and fears, then understanding hope and hopefulness in a variety of specific domains of human life will require us to understand the specific anxieties that motivate our hopes in these domains. I am not referring here only to worries and concerns that might be uppermost in our minds. As we saw when discussing hopefulness, many anxieties affect us on the pre-conscious level of our subjectivity. So which anxieties are especially germane to the domain of the healthcare clinic?

We live our lives with bodies that are vulnerable to a multitude of insults and injuries. From mild events such as stubbing one's toe or catching the common cold, to more dramatic events such as being badly injured in a car crash or contracting a serious disease, we are constantly reminded that our health and well-being are precarious. Moreover, we fear the pain and discomforts that often accompany injury or malady. We worry about the time lost and the opportunities missed while we are laid up at home or confined in hospital. Accordingly, we take precautions, our loved ones look out for us, our communities establish healthcare institutions and emergency services, and governments set aside huge proportions of their budgets for healthcare. And yet, we can never be certain that our health will not come under attack from either infection or trauma. We remain anxious. And so we entertain a general hopefulness that we will stay healthy. And when we are sick or injured, we hope that we will recover. Typically anyone who gets sick hopes to get better. Whether it is a headache or a serious illness, the condition is undesirable and we want to be rid of it. This leads to hope because we cannot completely control the outcomes when we seek treatment; even an aspirin is not guaranteed to rid us of a headache. There is a gap between what we are able to do and what we would like to achieve that generates uncertainty, and so we hope for relief. The threats of illness and injury, the fear of pain and suffering and the uncertainties of medical treatments are constant sources of anxiety.

But the deepest anxiety that affects us is the fear of death. I am not suggesting that we have this fear in the forefront of our minds as we go about our daily business. Indeed, most of us try hard to ignore this fear and to obliterate it from our consciousness. But at the level of the deeper motivational reaches of our subjectivity we have an unarticulated awareness of our deaths and from time to time we consciously think about it. Indeed, it has been suggested that we are the only worldly beings who think about our deaths. A being that only responds to stimuli that are immediately present to it –

whether it be food, shelter or a mate – can only be aware of those stimuli in the immediate time frame in which it is living here and now. It eats the food, enjoys the comfort provided by the shelter, or mates. Its enjoyment is present to it here and now and ceases when the stimulus ceases. Of course it can suffer disappointments and pain when its access to food, shelter or a mate is denied, but what it cannot do is anticipate such disappointments and enjoyments or regret their passing. The stimuli are either present to it or they are not. If it feels fear it is in the form of an inclination to flee from a present threat, and if it feels hope it is in the inclination to eat, rest or mate with a present stimulus. The stimulus must be present to it both in the sense that it is there in proximity to the organism and in the sense that it is in the same time frame as the organism. We are talking about an organism that cannot remember its past (although it can acquire behavioural traits from previous experiences) or anticipate its future (although instinct will cause it to flee from present dangers). Human beings are not such organisms. We have a sense of time. We can recall the past and we can anticipate the future and plan for it. All of our examples of hope in Chapter 1 have been cases in which the person who hopes is focusing on the future and the possibilities or challenges that it contains.

But we need to acknowledge that the one huge and inescapable possibility that our futures contain is our death. We are all going to die and we know it. Our futures also contain the possible deaths of loved ones and of strangers we might care about in a general way. These deaths will grieve us when they occur and so we fear them now when they are still in the future. But our own death is of an existentially different kind. It is the very cessation of our existence. At death all hope stops. While we do not normally hope for anything unpleasant in our futures, we can at least hope that when they occur we will bear them with fortitude or that we will learn from them and grow in wisdom. We can even hope that the deaths of others will have such positive effects on us, even while we do not hope they will occur. But our own deaths cannot be born with fortitude or be learnt from. While our process of dying could indeed be born with fortitude, death is the moment at which our life ends and our subjectivity ceases to exist. Leaving aside for the moment beliefs about a possible life after death, death itself must be thought of, not as a beginning or an opportunity, but as the end of being. This is not something to be hoped for. There may be people who are suffering terrible pain or distress who hope for death, but it is not the state of being dead that they hope for; it is the cessation of their suffering.

For many people death is something to be feared and this fear has the potential to cast a pall over life. There are people who think that, because their projects could be interrupted by death at any time, such projects are not worth committing to. On this view, death negates the value of anything we do because it makes the achievement of our goals and our enjoyment of it uncertain. In this way the thought of death can prevent our goals from being valued or enjoyed. And so we don't think about it. We ignore it and get on with our lives. Deep down, however, we know that we are temporal beings and that our time is short. We live our lives as directed towards a future that contains the fulfilment of our hopes and the realization of our goals and yet we also know that this future can be denied us at any time. On his way to the university, hoping that it does not rain and that he will do well in his studies, John could be struck by a car and killed. What good would his hopes be to him then? It would all be for nothing. This constant future possibility – that of our own deaths – casts us into anxiety and fear, albeit this is an anxiety and fear that is most often lived at that level of our subjectivity of which we are not fully aware. Death appears to us like a horizon of our life beyond which there is nothing to hope for. It is the end and culmination of all our hopes without being the object of any of them.

Many religious people do have hopes relating to their deaths, however. It is not that they hope to die, but rather that they hope for a new kind of life after their deaths. In this way death is seen as a gateway and becomes a kind of object of hope. But it remains true that hoping stops when death comes. Even if there were life after death, it is believed to be a life of perfect bliss and beatific vision and so there would be nothing in it to hope for. It could not get any better. And if it was a state of "nirvana" understood as peace and non-suffering then, again, there would be nothing to hope for. And a life of eternal perdition in hell would also leave us with nothing to hope for. So death is the end of hope even if there is life after death. If there is life after death it would be a life radically different from a human life. It would be a life without hope or hopefulness.

Bioethical issues

One of the most significant and widespread effects of being ill – aside from the pain and suffering that it brings with it – is that it makes one dependent on others. Whether it be family, friends or clinicians, one is inclined to give oneself over to the care of others. In the terms of our analysis of hope, this highlights the feature of supplication. As one hopes to get well, one sends out an appeal to others for help. But this stance of supplication can encourage dependency in the patient and paternalism on the part of the clinician. Paternalism in healthcare is the tendency of healthcare workers to make decisions on behalf of their patients on the grounds that they know best and are acting in the patients' best interests. If the patient adopts the role of a supplicant and relinquishes responsibility for their treatment to the doctor, then a paternalistic relationship can more readily develop between them. In the past doctors felt that it was so important not to destroy the hope of their seriously ill patients that they would avoid telling them just how bad their prognoses were. They would withhold bad news from their patients on the grounds that, if those patients did not know that their deaths were relatively imminent, they would continue to hope and "fight" for life. It was believed that patients without hope would often not cooperate with, or participate fully in, their treatments. In more recent times, this policy has been deemed a denial of the autonomy and even dignity of the patient. It is now felt that patients have a right to know their prognoses and that healthcare workers should have sufficient respect for them and confidence in them to suppose that they can handle knowledge of their dire condition.

Moreover, whereas it had been assumed that knowledge of impending death leads to hopelessness, it is now accepted that a dying person still has much to hope for aside from their survival. In a situation where a patient is ill, the future state that is most hoped for is a cure. Happily, most medical situations are of this kind and the relevant healthcare workers will focus on achieving that cure. But in cases of chronic illness or terminal illness, where no cure can be realistically offered, hope can still be encouraged. This does not mean that a physician should suggest a visit to Lourdes in order to seek a miraculous cure. Even if hope for a cure would not be realistic, the patient can be offered hope for relief from pain or discomfort. A person suffering chronic pain can hope for the caring attentions of others. A person facing death can hope to part from their loved ones without leaving any "unfinished business" in their relationships. They can hope to complete their projects or leave an inspiring legacy to their children. They can hope to stay alive long enough for a distant relative to visit them in time. Patients can be given something other than survival to hope for. There are many other matters that a patient may be uncertain or anxious about. Will their financial affairs be put in order? Will their loved ones be provided for? Will their achievements be remembered? These and many other concerns are issues about which the patient can entertain hopes and these hopes may well have the same therapeutic benefits as hope for a cure. While healthcare workers rightly focus on cure when it is possible and palliation when it is not, the needs and hopes of their patients extend well beyond these merely biological goals. Sensitive and caring healthcare workers will facilitate the achievement of this large range of hopes.

One of the stages that dying patients often go through is denial of their fates. They will refuse to believe that their deaths are imminent and hope for a complete cure. This would be a failure on their part to entertain hopes that are realistic. It would be the vice of presumption, which in this case consists in believing that, because they do not deserve to die, some powerful agency will intervene to prevent it. Acceptance is both a more virtuous and a more peaceful stance. But acceptance of death need not entail the absence of hope. One can hope for a peaceful death and for a good ending to one's life. And healthcare workers can contribute to the fulfilment of these hopes.

An example

That the role of hope in the face of illness and death is very complex is shown in a profound book entitled *How we Die* by the American physician, Sherwin B. Nuland. Nuland begins his discussion of hope in the clinic by reminding his readers that it is one of the most widespread tenets of the ethos of medicine that patients suffering from severe and incurable maladies must not be allowed to lose hope. Moreover, he says, the whole institution of medicine, with its hospitals, clinics, emergency services, high technology and medical, nursing and ancillary staff has the effect of assuring patients that they can place their hope in the doctors and health professionals who tend to their needs. The unfortunate result is that dying patients often "hope against hope" in the sense that they continue to hope for a cure even when every rational consideration indicates that none is available. It is even worse, says Nuland, when a clinician encourages such hope even though there is no basis for it in medical science or technology. It is almost inevitable that a patient, fearing the end of their future and thus of any hope, will seize on the possibilities that medical expertise offers even if, objectively, the chances of cure are very slim.

Some commentators on modern medicine speak of "techno-logical brinkmanship", in which doctors are tempted to try every new and even untested therapy or treatment in order to prolong the life of a patient. Doctors seem to need to feel that they are doing something, even if what they are doing holds little promise of improvement in the patient's condition or even relief from their pain and suffering. Even when a patient is in an irreversible coma and would die without artificial life support, there is a felt need to maintain that life support so as to maintain the last flickering embers of hope. Indeed, patients themselves, or their families, often demand this burdensome and often futile treatment because they do not want to give up hope or be seen to be doing so. Nuland warns against this approach and urges both patients and doctors to accept the inevitability of death when it comes. Even though modern society finds it difficult to accept death as an existential part of life, and even though it is one of the core objectives of the profession of medicine to preserve life and to find cures for disease, it must also be possible to accept death when it can no longer be postponed without causing greater suffering and hardship for all those involved: the patient, their family and the clinic itself.

And yet, on one occasion Nuland himself failed to heed this advice. He describes the terminal suffering of his brother, Harvey, who was dying of incurable bowel cancer. Harvey was undergoing terrible pain and his disease had made his body a source of horror to him. Nuland told him about some experimental chemotherapy procedures that might just help to relieve his symptoms and delay his death. He offered him hope. He admits that he made a terrible mistake. He knew that his brother was dying and yet he felt he could not take away his only hope. Nuland knew that he was acting in denial of the facts, but just as he wanted to give his brother hope so he was himself driven by a hope that a miracle might yet occur. It is not only patients who use the psychological strategy of denial to prevent their seeing that the end of their life is inevitable. Family members and some clinicians do the same. For them the most important thing is to keep hope alive, even in the face of undeniable facts.

Nuland also reports that many severely ill patients tend to give over their responsibility for their own lives to others. They feel the need to be cared for and to allow others to make crucial decisions for them. In the face of death, they are already withdrawing from life even as they hope for its continuation. And so Nuland found himself depended on by his brother and found himself making decisions on his behalf that, if his brother had taken a more autonomous role, he might not have concurred with. The experimental treatment was tried. It resulted in nothing more than greater misery and suffering, and a useless and painful prolongation of Harvey's dying agony. Nuland sums up his reflections on this story:

> In this high-tech biomedical era, when the tantalizing possibility of miraculous new cures is daily dangled before our eyes, the temptation to see therapeutic hope is great, even in those situations when common sense would demand otherwise. To hold out this kind of hope is too frequently a deception, which in the long run proves far more often to be a disservice than the promised victory it seems at first. (1993: 233)

In order to explore the implications of this story for our understanding of hope as evinced both by patients and clinicians, let us reflect on it using the features of hope that I listed at the end of Chapter 1 and which I argued in Chapter 2 applied also to hopefulness.

75

First, hope is motivated by felt needs or some degree of anxiety or concern, as opposed to fantasy or desire. In this case, the anxiety is all too clear. It is the anxiety evoked by impending death. Most people of sound mind do not want to die and in the face of death will cling tenaciously to life and to any means of preserving it. The deepest anxiety from which human beings suffer is the anticipation of death. As I noted in the previous section, even people in the best of health and at the peak of their powers cannot escape the occasional gnawing realization that death can come at any moment. Hope responds to this anxiety by clinging to life and hoping for its indefinite continuation. Or so it did for Harvey. For Nuland himself, the hope was that he could save his brother. Perhaps the anxiety that motivated this, apart from brotherly love, was the desire not to allow the science of medicine to be seen as inadequate to the task of saving life.

Second, hope implies a judgement that what is hoped for is something good. Whether what was hoped for in this case was judged to be something good will depend on whether we consider the matter from the point of view of Harvey or of Nuland. It is clear enough that Nuland, the physician, thought that the continued life of his brother would be a good, even if the duration of his continued existence would be short and the quality of it highly compromised and with no escape from suffering. For him the issue was that he wanted to give his brother hope. It is not so clear what Harvey thought. He might well have thought that a continuation of his suffering was not worth the effort and he might have hoped for its end. While Nuland did not do so himself, we could also imagine a healthcare worker thinking that a continuation of life was always a good thing irrespective of the quality of that life. The doctrine of the sanctity of life holds that life is always a good in and of itself, and that, therefore, doctors and patients have an obligation to prolong life or, at least, not to shorten it by any medical means. Moreover, given the professional commitment of healthcare workers to saving and prolonging lives, it is natural that such workers will be inclined to see saving and prolonging lives as a good thing. However, there is judgement required here and no overarching doctrine, such as that of the sanctity of life, should override such judgements. There are a number of goods that can be hoped for that we could sum up with the phrase "a peaceful death".

Third, hope's object is an occurrence that is considered to be possible. Harvey is made to believe – and indeed, wants to believe – that a cure is possible. All the indications are that it is all but impossible. However, it is the "all but" that is most important here. It provides the slight glimpse of a possibility that allows Nuland and his brother to still hope for what would be regarded as a miracle. However slight the chance, the depth of the fear of death turns that slight chance into a glowing light of possibility on which all the hope and longing of the dying patient is concentrated. It therefore becomes the clinician's task to be clear and honest about what is possible and what is not. While clinicians themselves can often not know with certainty what the prognosis of an illness might be, their professional knowledge can be of immeasurable help to the patient in shaping a realistic hope. Moreover, patients – perhaps helped by family, friends or clinicians – can explore the many other goals aside from survival that are still possible for them in their reduced state.

Fourth, hope's object is an occurrence that is considered to be not inevitable. In this story, the object of hope is the cure of Harvey's bowel cancer. Clearly such a cure is not inevitable. Despite all the expertise of the medical staff and the progress in medical research into cancer, the cure of Harvey's disease is, in fact, extremely unlikely. His chances of survival are vanishingly small. It is the huge gap between what Harvey and his brother want and the likelihood of its coming about that creates the space that hope seeks to fill.

Fifth, hope is directed towards the future as conceived by the person who hopes. This would seem an obvious point: the death that is feared and the cure or remission that is hoped for lie in the future. But there is a further significant point to be made here. When a patient is approaching death, it might be better to dwell on the past than on the future. It is the past that now holds the key to happiness. If the future holds little promise except suffering, it is time to reflect on the past: on the achievements that might lie there; on the loves and relationships that have enhanced it; and on the future legacy that will have been created. It is here that the clinician must concentrate less on survival and help the patient to come to terms with what needs to be done in order to secure a peaceful death.

Sixth, the person hoping is uncertain as to whether what is hoped for will happen. It is clear that uncertainty about whether or when a cure will come about is a condition for an ill person's hoping for that cure. If such a cure were certain all one would have to do would be to wait. In mild and non-terminal cases one might hope for an infection to go away or for an injury to heal sooner rather than later, but one knows that they eventually will. But this uncertainty condition is a source of difficulty for Nuland and other doctors. If they tell their patients that they will certainly die relatively soon as a result of their terminal illness they are said to be removing hope. And yet, if they do not tell them or if they offer them possibly futile treatments, they are said to be giving them "false hope". It seems that patients need some degree of uncertainty to leave room for hope but that this room must not be filled with unrealistic expectations. This is a quandary that all healthcare workers face.

Seventh, hope is directed to circumstances over which the person hoping does not have complete control. The most obvious element over which both Harvey and Nuland have no control is the progress of Harvey's disease. Despite the best efforts of the doctors, his cancer has spread to all parts of his body and has become incurable. He still has some control of the treatment regimen to which he is being subjected, but even here his hope is leading him to relinquish that to his brother and to his doctors. It is his lack of control over his own body and his health that is the most frustrating experience for him. Despite his hope for extended and healthy life, the disease is destroying him and his control over his own existence. And clinicians are also – despite the most sophisticated technological developments in medical science – unable to control all the permutations of the disease that is ravaging the patient. Even they often reach a point where all that is left to them to do is hope.

Eighth, hope ought to lead to appropriate action on the part of the person who hopes when such action is available. The urgent issue for Harvey is what action it is appropriate for him to take. Should he pursue the untested therapy or should he accept the inevitability of his death as peacefully as he can? His brother the doctor has suggested the new therapy. He himself has given over some of his responsibility for himself to his brother. As a result his ability to decide what action should be taken is severely compromised. The case also highlights how difficult it is for the clinician to know what would be the appropriate action to take.

Ninth, hope has the psychological structure of supplication. It is this point that throws the most interesting light on the story. Harvey, in his suffering and despair, had nowhere to turn but to his doctors and his brother. He was desperate for help. He hoped against hope that he would be cured or that his life would at least go on for somewhat longer without the terrible pain he was suffering. He appealed to his brother. It is not recorded whether he prayed to his god or sought help from any other agency. But his appeal to his brother was a palpable expression of his hope. It was because of this appeal and because of its intensity that his brother forgot the advice he had given to other doctors and offered a groundless hope. Harvey probably knew deep down within himself that his time was up but he hoped against hope and issued a supplication. He wanted some powerful agency to intervene in his life and perform a miracle. He gave up his responsibility for himself and gave himself over to his medically trained brother, whom he trusted to help him and even, miraculously, cure him. It is because clinicians are cast into the role of being the object of supplication that they carry such a heavy burden of responsibility.

And finally, hope ought to be rational and realistic. This is the crucial condition that would make Harvey's hope for a prolongation of his life legitimate. But we have seen that he was not being rational and realistic. He was seizing on an unlikely cure and a useless treatment in the vain hope that his life would be improved and lengthened. Of course, it must be admitted that his capacity for making a sound judgement in the situation that he was in was severely reduced. This is the reason why his physician brother accepted the responsibility and the blame for recommending a treatment that had no purpose except to maintain hope.

Conclusion

This story and the lessons I have drawn from it illustrate how hope might have both positive and negative consequences in cases where a patient is dying from an incurable disease or from severe injuries. However, for most people the medical clinic is a place where genuine and effective help can be obtained for a vast range of ailments ranging from the relatively trivial to the more severe and life-threatening. In such cases hope has a less problematic role to play. The patient hopes for relief from certain symptoms and the clinician provides the means in accordance with the best knowledge available. There is not as much room for drama where life is not under threat. Nevertheless, the structure of hope that I have identified in the case of terminal illness applies to less critical cases as well, especially the stance of supplication that the patient extends towards the clinician. Hope is an inescapable and problematic aspect of the experience of illness for patients, and also the source of many of the ethical dilemmas that healthcare workers face in the clinic.

4. Hope and politics

Politics is the social and institutional attempt on the part of a community to formulate, agree on and implement policies for the common good. Whatever corruptions it might be subject to – and there are many – its primary focus is on good governance and the maintenance of cultural, social and economic conditions that will allow people to live full and happy lives in accordance with the values they and their communities hold dear. Whether the structures through which decisions are arrived at and put into effect are democratic or autocratic, participatory or hierarchical, liberal or authoritarian, the professed aim of political processes is the improvement of the lives of those who are encompassed by that political system. Given this focus on the future, on amelioration and on corruptible structures of power and control, it is not surprising that hope should be a central element in politics. To adapt Ricoeur's thesis about the goals of our innate hopefulness to the political sphere, people engage in politics because they hope for improvements in their lives, for cooperative relations with others, and for stable and just social structures in which to live.

Barack Obama

Perhaps the most resounding statement of this role of hope has come from US President Barack Obama. In the Democratic National Convention keynote address that he delivered on 27 July

2004, at the Fleet Center in Boston, then Illinois senator Obama endorsed John Kerry and John Edwards as Democratic Party candidates for the presidency and vice-presidency of the United States, respectively. Towards the end of the speech he said:

> In the end, that's what this election is about. Do we participate in a politics of cynicism or do we participate in a politics of hope? John Kerry calls on us to hope. John Edwards calls on us to hope. I'm not talking about blind optimism here: the almost willful ignorance that thinks unemployment will go away if we just don't think about it, or that the health care crisis will solve itself if we just ignore it. That's not what I'm talking about. I'm talking about something more substantial. It's the hope of slaves sitting around a fire singing freedom songs; the hope of immigrants setting out for distant shores; the hope of a young naval lieutenant bravely patrolling the Mekong Delta; the hope of a millworker's son who dares to defy the odds; the hope of a skinny kid with a funny name who believes that America has a place for him, too. Hope in the face of difficulty. Hope in the face of uncertainty. The audacity of hope! In the end, that is God's greatest gift to us, the bedrock of this nation. A belief in things not seen. A belief that there are better days ahead.

The phrase "the audacity of hope" went on to become the title of Obama's book-length political manifesto.

There are many interesting points to notice about this speech. First, Obama is contrasting hope and cynicism in the way that, at the end of Chapter 2, I suggested Aristotle would have done. Political engagement is motivated by hope, which involves the belief not only that things can be better if action is taken, but that it is worth taking such action. The outcomes that political engagement seeks are worthwhile and important outcomes: the pursuit of justice in the distribution of social goods, economic prosperity, peace and security, the protection of the environment, and the alleviation of needless suffering both at home and abroad. These and the many other issues with which politics concerns itself are important and valuable goals. Hope not only pursues them with confidence but also believes in their importance. In is in this sense that cynicism – the feeling that nothing is important – is the opposite of political hope.

Political anxieties

Once again I can explicate what is involved in political hope by using my ten-point analysis from Chapter 1. First, political hope is motivated by felt needs or some degree of anxiety or concern, as opposed to fantasy or desire. The notable English philosopher Thomas Hobbes (1588–1679) created a myth to account for the origin of politics. He envisages pre-political human beings living on their own or in family groups eking out a living in a context of scarcity and therefore forced to both steal the necessities of life from others and to defend their possessions from the predations of their fellow human beings. Everyone has a right to survive and therefore to do whatever is necessary to do so. However, in this lawless, dog-eat-dog world, life is "solitary, poor, nasty, brutish and short" (*Leviathan*, ch. 13, para. 9), so the people decide to give up their right to look after themselves on their own and vest it in a ruler who will enforce cooperation between his subjects by force of arms and secure peace by the imposition of absolute power. Whether any such "social contract" was ever entered into as a historical event is doubtful, but the myth nicely captures the paradoxes and anxieties that infect politics. On the one hand, human beings are portrayed as self-seeking and violent. Leaving them to themselves to live in total freedom will lead to murderous anarchy. But on the other hand, political authority is portrayed as oppressive and coercive. Organizing people into a cooperative society with a ruler requires tyranny and despotism. These two extremes, anarchy and tyranny, are the objects of the political anxieties that inspire our political hopes and which have led some to describe Western political ideology as a "liberalism of fear".

The first such anxiety centres on freedom. We want to pursue our life's goals without undue interference from others and yet we also need government to maintain the law and exercise power on our behalf. Indeed, we need government for a host of reasons: to protect the borders, police the laws, establish the material and legal infrastructures for the pursuit of commerce, provide welfare support for those in need, ensure that there is education for all and healthcare for those who need it, regulate the financial system, protect the environment, support the arts, provide public amenities for sport and recreation, provide for transport, mail and electronic communications. The list goes on. But each of these functions requires institutions with rules and regulations that require cooperation from citizens, most obviously in the form of taxation, but as often as not in the form of having one's activities curtailed for the sake of the common good. If a modern nation state is a system of cooperation in order to allow people to secure common objectives and goods, it is also a system of coercion to secure that cooperation from everyone. In this way a reduction of our freedom is a price that has to be paid for the goods that governments provide. Our concern to protect our freedom is an anxiety generated by the institutions of politics themselves.

And there are other fears, anxieties and concerns for the resolution of which we look to politics. We want to be protected from foreign invasion, from crime and from terrorism. We want to be provided with the means to live and be helped when we are in need. We want opportunities to better ourselves. We want the wealth and goods that a society produces to be distributed fairly. We want to be recognized as having dignity and rights irrespective of which ethnicity, religion, language or gender our identity is based on. We want to feel that our identity is acknowledged and that the society in which we live embraces the cultures of all. We want to feel part of a community, its traditions and its aspirations, and to feel that the community we are a part of is respected by others. We want to feel that we are not powerless and that we can participate in the decision-making that affects our lives. We want our leaders to pursue our ethical goals – such as caring for the environment, providing for the global poor and maintaining world peace – on our behalf. We want our leaders to be able to secure this long list of goals and not to be hampered by special interest groups or political elites with vested interests. It is these and many other concerns and anxieties that lead people to look to politics and to politicians for solutions and for leadership. They lead people to entertain political hope.

I should add that the scope of government, and hence of politics, is subject to constant debate. Neoliberal ideologues would have governments withdraw from economic oversight, while religious fundamentalists would have governments legislate their moral preferences into law. However such debates play out, it is clear that what is at issue in politics is of concern to all those who are affected by the decisions that are taken. These matters are not just fantasies or idle desires that we might fulfil in private recreations or domestic life. We are concerned for others as well as ourselves. We all have an interest in what our governments do and we all feel some degree of concern or even anxiety about the policy issues that are debated and decided by those who hold political power.

The second feature of political hope is that we all hope that political decisions will be for the good as we see it. But it is important to notice that the judgement as to what political policies are good should not be made in the light only of self-interest. The person who votes for a particular political party because that party promises tax breaks that will be of private benefit to him does not understand that responsible politics is aimed at the *common* good. It may be necessary to sacrifice some private advantage in order to secure a public good. The judgement that what we hope for is something good should be an exercise of such political responsibility. It is a corruption of politics to see it as a competition between competing private interests rather than as a cooperative discourse aimed at a collective good. This is one reason why subsuming political goals and aspirations to the management of the economy – the sphere of competing private interests *par excellence* – constitutes a misunderstanding of the nature of politics. It is not a function of government to ensure that wealth flows only to those who contribute to the economy.

Third, political hope's object is an occurrence or a policy outcome that is considered to be possible. If we need to hope because social progress is not guaranteed, we are also led to hope by the belief that it is possible. But it is precisely at this point that the deepest quandaries of political hope arise. To the ordinary citizen and to the powerful politician alike, change for the better seems all but impossible. In the distant past a man's political and moral responsibilities might be confined to the village and his political action centred on local concerns. Provided he kept the peace, assured the harvest and harmed none of his neighbours, his political decisions could fulfil his every social hope and moral responsibility. Today, in contrast, we are aware that our actions and social policies have global impacts. We know that when we buy consumer goods we are complicit in the exploitation of millions of impoverished workers in the developing world. We know that when we eat we are encouraging distortions in global food production and trade that are causing starvation and environmental degradation in poorer countries. We know that whenever we travel, unless it is by foot or bicycle, we leave a carbon footprint that will endanger future generations through global warming. We know that when we pursue our national interests, we often generate global conflicts that have the potential to unleash wars of unimaginable destructiveness. We know that when we espouse the traditional or religious beliefs of our communities or our nations, we might encourage the ethnocentrism, intolerance and xenophobia that lead to a "clash of civilizations" and even terrorism. We know that the global political and economic institutions we have created to confront these problems, such as the United Nations and the World Bank, are compromised by national political interests and the greed of powerful elites. In the face of all this, what can an ordinary person do? What amelioration is possible? How can we avoid the vice of resignation? What scope is there for hope?

It is striking that in his speech accepting victory in the presidential election of 2008, Obama recited a litany of difficult political tasks and reforms and repeated after each one the refrain "Yes, we can!" This inspires hope. If he had identified cynicism as the opposite of hope in his earlier speech, he is now identifying despair as its opposite. Despair is the feeling that the task is too great and that success is too far out of reach. Such a feeling would lead to resignation: the belief that I am too weak and insignificant to achieve the goal. Obama's litany is an attempt to say otherwise. Change is possible, and hope for such change is therefore legitimate.

Fourth, political hope's object is an occurrence or a policy outcome that is considered to be not inevitable. What this means is that the future goods that politics aims for should not be considered to be decreed by fate, as it were. They should not be seen as the result of some historical process that no one can stop or influence in any way. To think this way would be presumption. Political goals have to be striven for. It is part of the structure of democratic politics that political decision-making is subject to many and competing influences. No matter how obviously good political goals may seem to their proponents, there will always be opposition from opponents who will be equally convinced of the justifiability of their position. Various points of view have to be taken into consideration and compromises have to be struck. When I participate actively in the political process by advocating particular policies, writing to newspapers, joining lobby groups and, of course, voting in elections, the outcome of my efforts is by no means guaranteed. Even an obviously good outcome is not inevitable. This is why political action needs to be motivated by a hope that acknowledges this contingency.

And yet political hope also seeks to overcome this contingency. Political rhetoric often seeks to hide it by appealing to overarching values and abstract concepts that have universal appeal but little specific meaning and that make the outcome seem inevitable. For example, politicians will advocate policies by claiming that they are consistent with the nation's destiny, or that they conduce to such grand goals as freedom, justice, economic growth or historical progress. They will say that their nation's endeavours must succeed because it has God on its side. But while all of these vague and romantic concepts obtain their rhetorical power from the hope that underlies them, they are a presumptuous distortion of genuine hope.

The idea of progress

Let us explore this claim with reference to belief in the inevitability of progress. In the distant past people thought that events occurred in historical cycles. In ancient agrarian societies, people were impressed by the regularity of the seasons. Just as day followed night so summer followed spring, which, in turn, followed winter and autumn. The seasons were especially important because the sowing and harvesting of crops, and thus the fruitfulness of the earth, were bound up with them. Thoughtful people discovered other cyclic regularities as well. The movements of the heavenly bodies were regular and cyclical and marked out the months and years. Historical epochs also came and went and the powers of kings and emperors waxed and waned in accordance with cycles deemed to have been laid out by heavenly powers. What all this amounted to was a conception of time and of history as cyclical. There was nothing new under the sun and human life proceeded along predetermined recurrent paths laid out by the gods.

But then in Europe in the sixteenth and seventeenth centuries, under the influence of the newly emerging sciences, the idea came to take hold that human beings might change the way they live for the better. They might harness the forces of nature that they had begun to understand scientifically by developing technologies. They might learn from the ancients, and from their own creative speculations, how to order the social and political lives of people in ways better than the mere use of force and coercion. In short, a new idea was emerging: the idea of "progress". No longer were human beings seen as confined to a temporal cycle in which they always did what had already been done. Human beings could invent new ways of doing things, new forms of political organization, new conceptions of the heavens and of supernatural entities, new bodies of scientific knowledge and new forms of artistic creation. Once this genie was out of the bottle there was no stopping it. Change in the name of progress became the central commitment of civilized people and their source of power and wealth over the whole of crea- tion, including subjugated peoples who were deemed to be unable to benefit from this progress. And the most important attitude that accompanied this new conception of progress was hope.

This period of European history is now known as the Enlighten- ment. It is the period in which human beings learnt to think for themselves. Rather than being caught up in traditional beliefs and practices, they considered themselves able to devise new ways of understanding the world and human history and to develop new conceptions of what a good life might consist in. In short, human beings became modern. Instead of conforming to traditions, religious norms or the ways of the ancestors, we became individualists convinced that we could choose our own ways of life and our own values. Instead of science having to conform to metaphysical beliefs inherited from religion, instead of social mores having to be sanctified by the Church and by theocratic tradition, instead of art being subject to the tastes of aristocratic patrons, instead of political life being subject to the hereditary power of kings and princes, human life would be progressive and free. What a glorious hope the Enlightenment gave to European civilization in the eighteenth century. Human kind was at last set free to pursue creativity, change and progress in every human endeavour.

Indeed, if we think of the changes we experience in our own lives today it is hard to escape the idea that progress is inherent in human history. Many of us can remember when flying in aeroplanes was an activity for daredevils or for an extremely rich minority. We can remember writing on typewriters and having to crank up our cars to start them. We wrote letters rather than sending SMS messages or talking on Skype. While progress is less obvious in spheres other than technology, there are many who assume that science is giving us ever-better knowledge and that political change is leading to evermore just and free societies.

But the idea of progress gives rise to a further thought. If there is progress, what are we progressing towards? If history is not cyclic but directional, then what is its goal? In the nineteenth century there were a number of important thinkers who suggested that the direction of history was predetermined by inherent influences and could be discovered by suitable social enquiry. Some argued that we were headed towards an inevitable rule of enlightened political leaders, others that Reason itself (spelt with a capital "R") was working itself out so as to create an enlightened society. Others again claimed that the political dominance of capitalism would be overcome by the working classes so as to usher in a new era of distributive justice in which the state would wither away. More recently it was suggested that biological and social evolution was tending to an "omega point" in which all the religious aspirations of humankind would be realized. Political liberals are inclined to think that, because their political philosophy is based on a universally valid conception of human dignity and reason, it will inevitably extend itself to the whole of humankind despite the strength of autocratic and theocratic governments in the world. What all these views have in common is that they take the element of contingency out of the concept of progress. They suggest that history is fulfilling a destiny. They deny the contingency of politics.

However, the idea of progress may be an illusion that hides the attempts of powerful elites to direct historical events in their favour. Nationalism, with its appeals to the destiny of a people and its justifications of war, colonialism, with its promise of spreading the purported benefits of civilization to allegedly primitive peoples, industrialization, with its exploitation of the working class and of natural resources, capitalism, with its enrichment of a few at the cost of the exploitation of millions, and consumerism, with its new forms of cultural emptiness, have all come to us in the name of progress. The world is marked by extreme differentials in wealth and millions are living below the poverty line and dying premature and avoidable deaths. The global conflicts of the twentieth century, along with the Holocaust and other instances of genocide, are also arguably products of the dreams that the Enlightenment gave rise to.

We should acknowledge that if there has been progress in human history then it is at least partly due to luck. It is not because of the working out of some cosmic, theological or metaphysical inevitability. Things just happen. If those things are positive in some way we seize on them and build on them. Some of these efforts succeed and others fail. We go on to develop the successes. And so it goes, ever onwards. But we could be building on failures as well, and our efforts could come to nothing. If the sum of all that we do turns out to be progressive then good luck will have played a considerable part. Liberal democracy is both a recent and vulnerable political form. Progress is not inevitable. It is because history is contingent in this way that we need to hope. If progress and improvement were inevitable or fated, we would only need to wait for things to get better. We might need to play our part, but we could be confident that the goods that politics promises would emerge in the fullness of time. Genuine hope does not think that way. It recognizes the contingency of history and the precariousness of the outcomes it produces: that *we* produce. That is why we need genuine hope: so that we can see through the rhetoric of politics and recognize that we need to act in order to reach the goals we aspire to.

The practice of politics

Returning to our list of features of hope, the fifth such feature is that political hope is directed towards the future as conceived by the person who hopes. This would seem obvious from what I have said so far and from Obama's reference to "a belief that there are better days ahead". The key political issues relate to policies and reforms that are oriented towards the future.

However, the past is also important in politics. The way in which citizens feel themselves to be members of the political community depends on their identification with the traditions and heritage of their nation state. Whether it is a society with a long ethnic and religious tradition or a settler society embracing peoples from many cultures, whether it a society that has won its independence in struggles for liberation against oppression or colonial rule, or whether it is a country of immense military and economic power that has defended democratic values in the face of totalitarianism, these are all aspects of a nation's past that affect the way people think about the present and the future. Accordingly, politicians have to deal with the past as well as the future. In Australia in 2008, then Prime Minister Kevin Rudd offered an apology to those aboriginal Australians who had been forcibly removed from their families in times past in order to hasten their assimilation into the white community. This policy had come to be seen as a grave moral wrong. It was appropriate for this gesture of reconciliation to be made in the political sphere even though it related to the past. We could also point to the Truth and Reconciliation Commission in post-apartheid South Africa chaired by Archbishop Desmond Tutu as a relevant example. Post-genocide criminal trials conducted by the United Nations are a further example. Although such gestures and institutions predominantly refer to the past, part of their importance lies in the future. They allow previously estranged and oppressed peoples to live together and to develop a common social life with those who had oppressed them.

It is striking that Obama refers to the past in his speech. His examples, although homely, remind his audience of the stories that – multiplied many times over – constitute the shared history of his people and thus the basis of their common hope for the future.

Sixth, it follows from everything I have been saying that participants in politics will feel that political outcomes are uncertain. Not only are many of the goals difficult to achieve, but the volatility of politics often means that when governments change, policies change with them and previous decisions are overturned. What is gained one year can be lost the next. Indeed, political decisions never seem to reach finality. To think otherwise would be presumption. As circumstances change adjustments need to be made and as ideas and ideals change, new policies are introduced. Nothing is ever settled. There is always a need for review. Moreover, the efforts of political actors can be easily negated as populist sentiment or vested interests achieve more or less influence over decision-making. Discouragement is the lot of the politically active. And yet, one must not succumb to resignation. Because the issues are so consequential, the effort must be made and determination shown.

Seventh, political hope is directed to circumstances over which the person hoping does not have complete control. Once again, it seems obvious that ordinary people, at least, have very little control over political outcomes. Even in revolutionary moments when people rise up against despotic rule, the outcome of the revolutionary movement is far from predictable or controllable and reactionary elites are quite capable of seizing their opportunity to introduce new forms of oppression and exploitation. But even the political elites themselves do not have complete control over the states in which they exercise power. Even the apparently most powerful man in the world, the President of the United States of America, is subject to a great many pressures and influences that curtail his freedom to introduce new policies. Congress can frustrate his every plan. Indeed, some degree of frustration is built into the system. The division of powers between executive, legislature and judiciary creates a safeguard against autocratic or illiberal rule. As well, the many powerful lobby groups, media moguls and vested interests that influence government policy through the power of money tend to corrupt even the most legitimate political processes. In the face of this, ordinary citizens can readily come to feel powerless in the face of political institutions despite their having, in democratic societies at least, guaranteed rights of political participation. But this sense of powerlessness should not lead to despair or resignation. Rather, it necessitates hope. Even if no one person can control political events, collective movements can have a considerable influence. Recognizing such limited but real power should be a strong stimulant for hope. I do not mean only that it can provide encouragement. I mean that because our political power is so modest, we need hope to fill the inevitable gap between what we are committed to achieving and what we can realistically achieve.

Eighth, political hope ought to lead to appropriate action on the part of the person who hopes, when such action is available. This thought leads to the advocacy of political participation. The minimal but necessary form of such participation is voting in elections. But a politically active citizen ought to do a lot more besides. She ought to inform herself of political debates so that her vote is cast responsibly. She ought to participate in political activities that fall outside the electoral process, such as writing to newspapers, joining advocacy groups or engaging in other legitimate ways of influencing government policy. What political scientists call "public discourse" is essential to political processes and everyone should find a way of participating in it either actively or receptively. It is an essential feature of democratic societies that they provide their citizens with opportunities to take actions of this kind, to express their political views, and to have a real and effective influence on the development of public policy by doing so.

The ninth point is that political hope has the psychological structure of supplication. This is clearly illustrated by the overwhelming excitement and joy that greeted the election of Barack Obama as US President in 2008. Many progressive and liberal voters would have seen the preceding presidency as fraught with political negatives and this would explain an element of relief at the election outcome. But the degree of expectation that the new president gave rise to was truly unprecedented. The words "hope" and "change" were bandied about in election slogans and the belief was encouraged that the new president could solve all the problems, both domestic and global, that had bedevilled the American republic in previous presidential terms. Obama became the object of supplication of a whole generation and of the African-American community. But as great a political breakthrough as Obama's success was, there was a significant lack of realism in the hopes that it inspired. There was a messianic element to it. Two years into his term, at the time of writing this book, the difficulties of the changes that

Obama promised have become all too plain. Nevertheless, it is to be expected that great expectations and high hopes will be placed in anyone who seems capable of delivering the kinds of social and political reform that many people crave. This is a quite understandable expression of that element of supplication that is present in hope.

However, there can be a dark side to this frame of mind. Many of the great demagogues and populist leaders of the past depended on this element of supplication in the hopes that people placed in them. Promising to save their people from oppression and exploitation, to bring an end to their humiliation and defeats, to restore the dignity and power of their race, to bring about the triumph of their religions and their morals, or to usher in a new millennium of justice and peace – albeit over the broken bodies of their enemies – has always been the modus operandi of fascist demagogues and populist rabble-rousers. If hope has as one of its constituent psychological elements the appeal to a higher power for secular salvation, then the influence of such leaders will be ever sustained. Hitler was seen by his supporters as the saviour of his people. The power of ruthless tyrants everywhere has been maintained, not only by terror and the suppression of dissent, but also by the trust and subservience of loyal followers who believed that their hopes for national glory or earthly paradise could be fulfilled by the actions of such leaders.

Even in more liberal societies, political rhetoric cannot avoid appealing to the hopes of the populace in similar ways. Political leaders seek to make themselves the object of the hope, supplication and trust of their followers in order to gain their allegiance and electoral support. A cynical or despairing reaction to political hope may well be a way of avoiding this problem, but it stymies action and commitment. Obama's rhetoric of hope illustrates this dynamic very well. By saying in his 2004 speech "As we breathe, we hope", he implies that it is a fundamental aspect of human nature to hope: an aspect that is expressed in the political process itself. For all its dangers, such political rhetoric is a call to action and encourages people to renewed efforts to change society for the better. Accordingly, while we should acknowledge the political dangers posed by hopes that place too much trust and faith in popular leaders, we cannot avoid accepting hope as an essential constituent of the modern political process.

The tenth and last point is that political hope ought to be rational and realistic. This means not only that goals should be realistic and achievable but also that citizens are required to contribute to political debates in terms that others can understand as relevant. It would be ineffective to argue for environmental controls, for example, on the grounds that the "Great Earth Spirit" commands it of us. These are not terms that are suitable to political debates in modern societies. Such an argument would not be deemed rational. Again, it is no good joining a debate on the high level of executive salaries, for example, by claiming that private property is theft and that we should all revert to a communal form of life in which everything is shared equally. In the context of modern society, such claims would be irrational and unrealistic.

However, this is a difficult norm to specify completely. Political action, especially when it is directed against entrenched interests or policies, ought to be bold and imaginative. When the vast majority of a political community agrees on a particular policy, those few who raise their voices against it – even on reasonable grounds – will often be deemed irrational and unrealistic. Opposition to the war in Vietnam, for example, was at first confined to a small minority who were deemed to be out of touch with geopolitical realities. Yet the movement they started grew in strength and eventually prevailed. No leader today wants to repeat that kind of military commitment. Was that anonymous man who stood firm against the tanks during the Tiananmen Square massacre in June 1989 failing in the virtue of hope because he was not being realistic? Was he being presumptuous or overly naive? To go further back in history, those few concerned citizens of Great Britain who began to oppose the international slave trade in the eighteenth century were seen as hopelessly irrational and unrealistic. Slavery was too much a part of the economic arrangements on which the wealth of many nations depended. And yet their struggle was eventually successful. No one today would even consider making slavery legal again. Indeed, the anti-slavery campaigners invented new ways of engaging in politics. Action committees, letters and submissions to parliament, boycotts, pamphleteering, and public agitation and demonstrations were all methods pioneered by this movement. Accordingly, we must not allow the requirement that we should be "realistic" to derail our legitimate commitments.

And yet there is a danger in this espousal of vision, imagination and boldness in pursuing a political cause. It becomes easy to fill one's head with grand visions of social change. It is easy to become "utopian" in one's thinking, especially if one has adopted the idea of progress and its corollary, the idea of a goal in history. In its earliest forms, utopian thinking consisted in imagining a society in which all social divisions and dissensions were absent. It took considerable imagination and literary skill to devise descriptions of such forms of life that could be believable, but a small literary genre was created that had some influence on political thought. Such utopian thinking is an expression of hope. However, it can happen that political activists are so fired up by their utopian visions of a future society in which all social ills are overcome that they are prepared to take extreme steps in bringing such a society about. Revolutionary movements are especially prone to such excesses. While revolutions are often justified by the oppression and exploitation to which they are a response, it can also happen that the fervour of the revolutionaries is fed not only by their resentment against oppression but also by their adherence to utopian ideologies in which new societies are imagined of such happiness and grandeur that no sacrifice is deemed too great to bring them about. Added to this it might be thought that such a future glorious society is guaranteed by destiny and that it is the historical task of the revolutionary vanguard to act boldly to bring it about. The Terror that followed the French Revolution and the victory of the Bolsheviks in the Russian Revolution are but the most dramatic examples of this tendency. During the height of the Stalinist period in the Soviet Union, millions of peasants and others who were deemed enemies of the revolution were sacrificed in the name of the communist ideal of a society of equality in which the state will have withered away. Nor is this tendency confined to examples from the past. The military and diplomatic actions of Western powers in the world today are often motivated by the hope of bringing democracy and liberal political rights to nations that currently do not enjoy such social conditions. This too would be an example of sacrificing the lives of some in order to pursue utopian hopes. Of course, it is true that many of these policies are motivated by a complex array of political and economic anxieties, including, for example, the need for secure access to highly prized natural resources. But such complexities only show that the deep strands of hope in utopian ways of thinking are not only dangerous but can also be misleading.

Some utopians can sustain their hope only by turning away from the evils of this world in disappointment, and pursuing a vision of radical change. The temptation is to want to sweep everything aside. Let's have revolution! Let's do away with the state! Let's overthrow the system! Let's bomb the oppressors out of existence even at the cost of our own lives! Let's create a truly murderous gesture! This way of thinking has spawned many radical movements throughout history and may be an inspiration for some acts of terrorism today. Prophets and preachers have promulgated apocalyptic or messianic ideas since time immemorial. Apocalyptic visions involve the destruction of the world as we know it and its replacement – usually at the hand of a supernatural force accompanied by cataclysmic events – with a new world in which the elect who are saved will live on in glory into the future. This way of thinking is also central to messianism, which is the belief shared by many world religions, including Judaism, Christianity and some branches of Islam, that a saviour will come and raise imperfect creation to a new level of spiritual and material development. Although we tend to think of salvation today as a personal destiny for each individual, it has often been thought of in the past in collective terms so that a whole people is saved because of its righteousness, while the communities of evil and unbelieving ones are swept away into eternal perdition. Millenarianism is the view that at "the end of days" evil will be swept aside and the reign of a new order lasting for a thousand years will be inaugurated. Some believe in the coming of the "Rapture", when the world will be destroyed, the good saved and infidels condemned. Even today there are religious fanatics in many faiths who hope for a second coming of some kind or who are preparing to build a new temple to their returning gods. Bizarre as some of these views may seem today, political ideologies can sometimes share such messianic visions. Political thinkers have dreamt of the perfect society and have been prepared to pursue their own versions of Armageddon in order to bring about this secular form of salvation on earth.

Conclusion

So what role can there be for a more rational and realistic hope? There can be no generalizable rules or principles on this issue. Sensitive and courageous judgements have to be made on the specifics of each situation. Sometimes a grand and heroic gesture is what is needed, but in most contexts, to be realistic is to acknowledge uncertainty and to work for achievable change. This may be less dramatic and the outcome might be less than the rule of the righteous over the whole of creation, but a slight improvement in even one life or a new possibility developed and achieved in even a small part of the world is still worthwhile. It is not acceptable to sacrifice achievable goals on the altar of grand visions. Of course, the judgement as to what is achievable has to be made in the context of difficult and complex situations and it has to be sensitive to deep human values. Perhaps when the history of Obama's presidency is written, it will be seen to have illustrated this point even if the sometimes messianic hopes he inspired remain unfulfilled.

5. Hope and religion

I have argued that hopefulness is a fundamental existential structure of human existence and that specific and episodic hopes are expressions of this primordial hopefulness. Perhaps the most obvious evidence for this claim is the phenomenon of religion. Statistics gathered in 2005 indicate that there are 2.1 billion Christians in the world (33 per cent of the world's population), 1.5 billion Muslims (21 per cent), 900 million Hindus (14 per cent), 394 million adherents of Chinese traditional religions (6 per cent), 376 million Buddhists (6 per cent), and many other religious adherents besides. Those who describe themselves as non-religious constitute just 16 per cent of the world population and almost half of these still describe themselves as "theistic". I regard these statistics as evidence for our primordial hopefulness because I consider religion to be an expression of that hopefulness. In this chapter I hope to justify this conviction and spell out its implications.

Spiritual anxieties

Like hope in other domains, religious hope is motivated by various needs, anxieties and concerns rather than mere fantasies or desires. Our lives are fragile, vulnerable, fallible and mortal. These and many other features of the human condition generate deep anxieties and concerns at the core of our being. As I noted in Chapter 3, it is our mortality that is the most pervasive source of dread and anxiety in our lives. We shall explore presently how religion has helped us face that dread, but outside a religious context we can only think that death will bring us oblivion. It is the end of our existence. For all we know the state of being dead is exactly like the state of not-yet-being-born. It is a state of non-existence that we can neither imagine nor remember. The total absence of conscious-ness makes such a state a complete nothingness. And this fills us with dread. Moreover, death can threaten the meaningfulness of our lives. Any project that I engage in can be frustrated by death at any time. The more worthy and the more difficult a project is, whether it be the creation of a fine work of art or the completion of important scientific research, my involvement in it can be snuffed out at any moment by untimely death. How, then, can this project be held to be so important? In the face of death it becomes difficult to be committed to any significant project. This thought threatens to make our lives meaningless.

Indeed, the quest for meaning in our lives can be a further spir-itual anxiety from which we all suffer. As we contemplate the vast-ness of the universe and the apparent limitlessness of time, we can consider our own existence to be puny and insignificant. Moreover, the world we live in is full of change, uncertainty and danger. Things can go wrong. We can be injured or frustrated in many ways. We have to wrest a living from this earth by the sweat of our brows. Can we feel at home in such a world? Is it a vale of tears in which we are tested for our worthiness of being happy, or is it the place where we belong and beyond which we have nothing to hope for? As we ask ourselves why we make the efforts we do and wonder whether it is all just a matter of eating, working, sleeping and defecating and then doing it all again day after day – even if it is enlivened by joy and love from time to time – we can easily be led to the thought that it is all meaningless. Albert Camus' (1913–60) famous image of the ancient Greek mythical figure Sisyphus comes to mind here. For offending the gods, Sisyphus was condemned for all eternity to the task of pushing a large boulder up a hill, only to have it roll down again so that he has to push it back up, and so on indefinitely. Camus presents this as an ultimately meaningless existence and as a metaphor for modern human life. In the face of such meaninglessness we have to create our own purpose in life. Although Camus did not advocate this, many of us hope to be part of something more significant than everyday life.

We also want to believe in morality. What bad people do – whether it be robbing, killing or raping other people – fills us with dread and loathing and so we condemn it as morally bad. But is this just an expression of our fear and loathing, or is it a judgement based on some rational moral reality? Is it just that we disapprove of them, or are such actions really wrong in themselves? That we might not have an answer to these questions also fills us with anxiety. We want our moral beliefs to be soundly based so that they can be enforceable and provide the touchstone against which the moral quality of a human life can be measured.

We are curious but fallible beings. We engage in the pursuit of knowledge and understanding not just in order to give ourselves technological control over nature but also to answer deep questions about the very nature of reality. Why is there something rather than nothing? What is the origin of the universe? What, if anything, lies beyond it? Does time have a beginning or an end? Because we are beings who can reflect on being, we cannot avoid thinking about the very origins of being. (The word "being" should be read as a verb in these last two iterations.)

We wonder too about beauty. The transformation of our environment through technology, and our mundane everyday lives with our regimens of work, rest and pragmatic concerns, seems to leave little room for beauty. And yet we crave it. Whether in the form of wild nature or in the form of art, we need the enrichment that beauty can bring. Even our popular entertainments take us into a realm of the imagination, mythology and meaning that enriches our lives and without which we would suffer cultural impoverishment.

And we are also anxious about our identities. I do not mean that we have doubts about the name and other details that appear on our passports or driving licences. I mean that we need a sense of belonging in our communities. We need to know who we are in terms of our ethnicity, religious affiliation, nationality, language group or gender. We need to know that our identity is respected by others. I have already mentioned this in the context of our political anxieties, but this is also a spiritual anxiety in the sense that it strikes at the very depths of our being. Our belonging to the community in which we live is not just a matter of being accepted as a functional contributor to that community or of being loved by other members of it – especially our families. It is also a matter of our feeling an identification with the stories and traditions of that community, with its beliefs, rituals and practices, with its language and customs. Our communities define who we are.

Because we are fragile and vulnerable we also need healing. By "healing" I don't just mean health and the healthcare services that would maintain it. I have discussed these in Chapter 3. I now allude to a deeper notion of healing or health captured by the, admittedly vague, notion of "wholeness". It is not insignificant that the words "health", "healing" and "wholeness" have the same etymology. We are not only anxious about our physical health and wellbeing in the sense of the absence of disease or injury; we also want to be strong and capable. Again, there is more to this than just the physical dimension. We want to be internally strong. We don't want to be in conflict with ourselves and be controlled by unruly appetites. We are anxious about our spiritual health and wellbeing. This might take the moral form of being concerned about not being guilty of any moral failures or of being virtuous in the ways that our communities admire, or it might take the aesthetic form of being at peace with oneself and noble in the way one presents oneself to the world.

We are anxious to be free of such spiritual ailments as vices, fears, hatreds and resentments: a form of freedom that, once again, takes us beyond the political sphere.

We are also anxious not to be alone. I do not mean just that we do not want to be isolated and that we want to have the company of others around us. It is possible to be spiritually alone even in a crowded room. We need connection with others. We need acceptance and love. We need to feel understood in what we think and even admired in what we do. Most of all we need someone to be the object of the supplication that I have argued is implicit in hope. It is when others meet these needs and respond to our anxieties in this way that we can be said to be truly happy.

Last, we are anxious about justice. I suggested in Chapter 2 that our fundamental quest in life was to live well, with and for others, in a society marked by justice. If this is right then justice is a deeply held value, the possible denial of which, either for ourselves or for others, fills us with dread. We don't want to be treated unfairly. The idea of justice here connects with that of morality. We think it just if good people prosper and bad people do not. If we see bad people flourishing we are inclined to think that things are not ordered as they should be. Somehow those bad people must get their comeuppance. The quest for justice is also a response to human suffering. We find it hard to accept the thought that suffering can be undeserved or that it cannot help us attain a just reward. Suffering would seem to be without purpose and it strikes anyone as if by chance. Surely it must be part of a system in which those who suffer without apparent reason are recompensed.

The central characteristic of these anxieties – and the reason I call them spiritual anxieties – is that they take us beyond our everyday practical existence. They take us beyond our pursuit of everyday needs and projects: our jobs, families and friends. We are not now concerned with earning a living or cleaning leaves out of our gutters but with finding meaning and depth in our lives. In this sense, what we are focused on is transcendence: the overcoming of the everyday. The notion of "transcendence" can be used to describe the objects of our innate and pre-conscious hopefulness. But in so far as our hopefulness is pre-conscious and pre-intentional – in so far as we are not fully aware of the objects it is directed upon or the goals it pursues – we can only use this term as a vague signifier to gesture towards the inchoate objects of our spiritual quest.

Metaphysical hope

However, many people and many cultural traditions are not satisfied with this vagueness. They want to give specificity, concreteness and a firm reality to these objects. And so they create metaphysics. The word "metaphysics" comes from the ancient Greek terms "*meta*", meaning "beyond", and "*physis*", meaning "matter". So the term refers to any object of thought or emotion that is taken to be beyond this physical and material world in some way. Philosophers use the term in a variety of technical ways, but I use it to refer to entities whose existence cannot be apprehended with our ordinary senses or by our rational understanding. Such entities might include ghosts, angels, souls and fairies, as well as non-personal entities or forces such as the influence that astrology claims the stars have on human personality. In his 2004 speech, Obama referred to "a belief in things not seen". He did not say what he meant but, given the depth of religious faith present in much of American society, we can assume he was referring to events produced by the providence of God. In speaking of metaphysical hope, therefore, I am seeking to understand the kind of hope that many people place in such supernatural entities as God, or angels, or a life after death.

Once again it will help to refer to a specific example. It concerns that great philosopher of ancient Athens Socrates (469–399 BCE). He has been condemned to death on a charge of trying to disabuse young people of their traditional beliefs in the gods. He is in prison and will soon be given hemlock to drink, a potion that will kill him. He is surrounded by a number of friends, including Cebes and Simmias, whom he has been trying to comfort with rational arguments in favour of the immortality of the soul. As well he has tried to reassure them that, despite the condemnation it has brought him, the life of philosophy is a noble and worthy one. And then this highly rational man, who has indeed used reason to cast doubt on the ancient mythologies of Athens, engages in a most remarkable speculation about the destiny of his soul after death. He describes a wondrous world in which the air is pure, the forests glorious and the waters clean. There are rivers of fire, water and mud and the souls of the departed are ushered by guardian spirits to those waters and lakes that they deserve as reward or punishment for the way they have lived their lives. The souls of those who have made wisdom their goal will live in beautiful mansions and will commune with others of similar spirit, unconfined and elevated. And then he says something so important as to be worth quoting in full:

> The reasons which we already described provide ground enough, as you can see, Simmias, for leaving nothing undone to attain during life some measure of goodness and wisdom; for the prize is glorious and the hope great. ... Of course, no reasonable man ought to insist that the facts are exactly as I have described them. But that either this or something very like it is a true account of our souls and their future habitations – since we have clear evidence that the soul is immortal – this, I think, is both a reasonable contention and a belief worth risking; for the risk is a noble one. We should use such accounts to inspire ourselves with confidence; and that is why I have already drawn out my tale so long.
>
> (*Phaedo* 114b–115c)

Soon after this, Socrates bathes, drinks the poison and dies.

What are we to make of this story? Some elements of it are familiar. The idea that good souls are rewarded after death and that bad souls are punished in ways commensurate with their faults is an idea taught by most of the world's great religions. Socrates uses this thought to justify the love of goodness and wisdom that marks the life of a philosopher. Moreover, the hope that Socrates entertains is given a specific and concrete object; namely, continuing existence in a beautiful place reserved for those who have attained wisdom. But what I am most struck by is the way that Socrates openly admits that he holds such beliefs in order to give himself confidence. He is sustained by his hope that his life of seeking wisdom will not now be negated by death but will rather be rewarded in a new form of life. There is no worldly evidence to support this hope. He is aware that his story is just that: a story. He has no empirical evidence or rational warrant for its truth and he knows that the accounts given by the ancient poets and oracles are no more reliable than his own. And yet he tells his friends this story in order to comfort them and to reassure himself. He holds that such beliefs are true because he hopes they are true. However, he is not lying. He does not consciously assume that the stories are false. He genuinely takes them to be true. But he also knows that it is his hope that makes them seem true to him. He knows that he is taking them to be true because to do so is a risk worth taking. Without evidence to support the story – or to deny it – he finds a reason to believe it in the thought that it is a good belief to have. It encourages people to live well and it provides comfort as they face their deaths. So it is reasonable to take it to be true. This is hope rather than evidence providing a foundation for belief.

Socrates is not the only philosopher to have based his faith on hope. Blaise Pascal (1623–62) considered that the question of whether God exists was not amenable to rational proof. Accordingly, he asks not whether it is true that God exists, but what is at stake in holding such a belief. What is at stake, he says, is our eternal life in heaven. If we believe in God and live morally, we will be rewarded, whereas if we do not believe – even if we live well – we will earn eternal damnation. It is, therefore, best to wager on the belief that God does exist. If God does indeed exist, eternal life will be available to us while, if we do not believe, it will be denied us. And if God does not exist there will be no eternal life in his presence no matter what we believe or how virtuously we live our lives. So nothing will be lost if we do believe in him. Accordingly, to secure eternal life, the best bet is to believe in God's existence. And so Pascal believes. Here once again we can see that it is his hope for eternal life that drives his decision to believe.

Kant also argued for the existence of God on the basis of hope. Having established what morality requires of us on the basis of pure reason and rationality, Kant then wonders what point there is in obeying the moral law. While we can know what the law requires of us on the basis of our own human reason, we also need some motivation to obey that law. This motivation can come, says Kant, from the thought that God will reward those who are good and punish those who are bad. Unless we have this thought there would be no point in being moral and our hopes for just rewards and punishments would be futile. Accordingly, Kant concludes that it is rational to believe in a God who is a just judge. Kant's hope for moral justice leads him to faith in God.

Another philosopher to have raised such issues is Søren Kierkegaard (1813–55). He too was troubled by the question of faith. Could it be based on either rational considerations or empirical evidence? Whenever he considered the teachings of the Christian religion, its doctrine of the incarnation and its narrative of the life of Jesus, he could see nothing but absurdity and contradiction. It made no sense to him and yet he wanted to commit himself to belief in it. Accordingly, he argued that such belief was based on a sheer leap of faith: a blind commitment that was not driven by any argument or proof. It was simply a step that one took out of the depth, longing and hope in one's own being: out of one's subjectivity. And it was a step that needed to be constantly repeated so as to avoid despair. For Kierkegaard, hope, as the opposite of despair, drives and creates faith. For him, too, hope is a basic existential structure of our being on which our faith is based.

One might object that there is something dishonest about these ways of thinking. If there is no evidence or rational argument for God's existence, then to decide to believe because one hopes that he exists is irrational. And if one's decision is motivated by hope for eternal reward, it is selfish and inauthentic. We shall come back to this complaint.

Hopefulness as a basis for faith

What I am suggesting is that metaphysical beliefs in supernatural entities such as God, life after death and eternal salvation are the products of our hopefulness. This is highly relevant to the under-standing of religion. Because of our spiritual anxieties we all yearn for transcendence and meaning. But religion comes into being only when this transcendence is transformed into metaphysical entities. In response to our anxieties about death, for example, knowing that we cannot live in the biological sense for ever, we come to believe that there is a metaphysical life after death. It might be an individual existence of spiritual rapport with God, or it might be a bodily resurrection into a new form of collective life. It might be reincarnation into a form of life commensurate with the amount of merit we have acquired in a previous life. It might involve many mansions and the enjoyment of unimaginable sensual delights. But it will not be the end. And that is the key point. We cannot face the thought that death is the termination of our existence in any form. So we hope for something more and that hope allows us to interpret the legends and myths of the past as assurances that we will live on.

In response to our anxiety about Sisyphian meaninglessness, we posit a God who gives us a purpose and a destiny in life. Being told that we are made in the image of God and have a glorious destiny with him in heaven can make even the most humble worldly existence seem worthwhile. In the context of political ideology rather than religion we might posit a purpose to history or to our nation, class, or race so that we can feel ourselves part of something more grand and noble than our puny, everyday existence. I had already begun to explore such metaphysical hope in some of the remarks I made about political hope in Chapter 4. In so far as political hope can take messianic and millenarian forms, it is well on the way to becoming metaphysical and religious in nature. Such hopes can also be a response to our quest for meaningfulness in our lives. In either a political form or a religious form, we come to see our lives – with all their apparently trivial concerns – as the fulfilment of a historical or divine destiny. Those of us who are religious might think that we are sent to this vale of tears in order to try us, and for us to earn our eternal reward in heaven. Or we feel we are adding to the glory of God through our good deeds or by accepting his will. Or we are fulfilling the law of karma, or achieving our release from the cycle of suffering through spiritual enlightenment. Whatever theology we believe in, the upshot is that our lives become meaningful. Moreover, we begin to see the world as where we ought to be. We do not quite see ourselves at home in the world with all its changeableness and uncertainty, but we do understand it as the anteroom to salvation in which we have a part to play and a destiny to fulfil.

In response to our need for an objective and enforceable morality, thinkers have been led to hope for a universal, objective and absolute set of moral norms. We have edifying stories such as that of God handing down the Ten Commandments to Moses. Socrates' pupil Plato posits a metaphysical order of Absolute Goodness, which we must all participate in to be virtuous. Kant argues that our pure reason cannot but disclose to us what we are commanded to do by the moral law. In these and many other ways we have tried to allay our anxiety that anything might be permitted or that what the powerful can get away with will have to be deemed acceptable by the rest of us.

In response to our fallibility and our quest for understanding, we hope for an objective and unassailable realm of truth. This hope led Plato to interpret the world of change and uncertainty as a pale copy of a more perfect world in which everything conformed to its essence and remained unchanging and clear for all time. The task of philosophy was to liberate the mind from this changeable and misleading world so as to see reality in the light of Truth (spelt with a capital "T"). It led Christian philosophers and theologians to interpret sacred scripture as the unerring word of God, giving us infallible revelation about himself and even about the natural world. Scientists such as Galileo Galilei (1564–1642), who dared to think for themselves and challenge the orthodoxy taught by the Church, were forced to recant under threat of torture. It led modern philosophers such as René Descartes (1596–1650) to posit a single indubitable proposition – "I think therefore I am" – from which all further certain knowledge, including of the existence of God, could be deduced. It led Kant to interpret knowledge as based not on our fallible senses alone, but on the operation of rational faculties that could guarantee the reliability of that knowledge. And today we still look to science to give us indubitable knowledge. However, science only ever gives us the empirically best explanation that is available in the context of current methodological best practice and of the most advanced experimental equipment. For technical, logical reasons, this does not amount to proof. And so, even today, many of us are driven to metaphysics in order to attain certainty. An example of this would be the idea that the universe was created by an intelligent designer such as God. Because we find it hard to accept the uncertainty that is endemic in scientific theorizing, and because we want to feel at home in this world, and because we find it so difficult to conceive of an infinity of time, we posit a creator who brings the universe into being and creates everything in it, including intelligent life.

Religion has always been a very effective response to our need for beauty. Some of the greatest architectural wonders of the world have been temples, mosques, cathedrals or other places of worship. Tombs such as the pyramids of Egypt or the Taj Mahal have spoken not only of respect and love for the dead but also of the profound religious beliefs of those who built them. Sacred music and the choreography of liturgical rites and ceremonies have added aesthetic depth to the lives of people of all classes and levels of education, and the stories told by religious teachers have elevated them above their ordinary concerns and sufferings. While these art forms do not contain any metaphysical elements within themselves – they are, after all, the product of merely human creativity and inspiration – they do point to a transcendent realm of meaning and they reinforce belief in the metaphysical entities posited by the religious traditions of which they are a part.

For all the billions of people who are religious, their faith is a crucial component of their identities. Their religious community is the focus of their sense of belonging. They secure their identity and sense of belonging by participating in the rituals, practices and beliefs of their religion. They share the worldview and the metaphysical beliefs of their community. They dress in accordance with its dress codes and eat in accordance with its dietary rules. Priests, gurus and shamans are clothed in ritual vestments and wash their hands and feet before engaging in the sacred rites. There is much debate these days about how women in Islamic communities should dress. Questions could be asked also about why Jews and Muslims shun pork while Hindus refuse to eat beef. There is no rational reason for these practices. In the case of the dietary rules, there are no nutritional or hygienic benefits to be gained. So why do people adhere to these practices? My theory is that it is a matter of affirming one's identity and sense of belonging to the relevant religious community. This is why it matters so much. If it were a rational matter, one could make the occasional exception or compromise on the issue if something of greater importance was at stake. But this does not happen. People would rather die than violate the relevant norms. Is this a matter of fanaticism or other forms of irrational pathology? No, it is a matter of affirming one's identity. Once again, this is not directly a metaphysical issue but, given that it is one that goes beyond instrumental reason and pragmatism, it is not surprising that it is supported by beliefs that also go beyond everyday rationality.

Most people today go to doctors or other suitably qualified practitioners when they suffer ill health. The fact that many people seek "alternative medicine", however, indicates that the matter may be more complicated than it seems. We seek not only relief and cure, but also other kinds of comfort. While it may be just that alternative practitioners give us more of their time, we may also seek their help because we recognize that healing is more than just a physical matter. Indeed, for by far the greatest part of the history of humankind, and still in many places today, illness is a spiritual matter and what people seek when they are ill is "healing" in the fuller sense I have already described. Witch doctors and shamans are only the most obvious examples of the combination of religion and the healing arts that many people still believe in, and which was the norm in most religions in pre-modern times. Jesus was known as a healer, and gurus of various traditions have cured physical ailments by helping patients become one with their feelings and emotions. Catholics travel to Lourdes and other shrines and pray to their favourite saints in the pursuit of miraculous cures for their maladies. These practices are based on metaphysical beliefs in supernatural powers that will intervene in human and physical events in order to provide cures.

But there is more than physical cures at stake here. Our sense of being well or whole is also connected to our moral standing in relation to God. We want to be forgiven our sins. We want to be in a state of grace. We want to advance in the cycle of reincarnations towards enlightenment. We want to feel that the spiritual powers are on our side. It is clear that metaphysical beliefs are central to these anxieties. We even posit supernatural gifts such as "grace" in order to articulate our understanding of these matters. In the realm of interpersonal and social relations we have such notions as that of "fault" or "crime", but the notion of "sin" is one that takes us beyond the realm of the everyday. It makes an inescapable reference to the gods and seeks, through rituals such as that of the Catholic confessional, a complete and secure solution to our spiritual anxiety to be healed.

Religion also overcomes our loneliness. At a worldly level, it provides communities of faith through which we can form friendships and fellowships with like-minded people. Religions are communities. But at a more metaphysical level, they provide even more. They give us divine friendship. Most major religions teach love and compassion and promise the love and compassion of God for us. This ensures that the overcoming of our loneliness is not jeopardized by the fickle and changeable nature of human relationships. How comforting it is for a Christian to know that "Jesus loves me".

In response to the inescapability of our suffering, some religions teach that we should seek spiritual enlightenment and an eventual escape from mortal existence. Others teach that we will be recompensed in the next life to the extent that our suffering in this life was not deserved. The key point here is that the next life – whatever form it takes – will be a life without suffering. But there is another important point here also. What we are hoping for here is not just release from suffering, but also justice. We think it is unfair when we suffer without deserving to and we hope for redress, if not in this life, then in the next.

Justice

The mention of justice here is very important. When we hope for a better society or for a blessed eternal life, what we are hoping for deep down is justice. This is a noble hope but it can quickly take the excessive forms of being metaphysical or unrealistic. Knowing that this world is often not just – that evil people flourish while the righteous suffer hardship, and that natural disasters strike at the guilty and the innocent alike – we appeal to a metaphysical order in which justice can be found. We can discern such an appeal in the beliefs of the ancient Greeks, for example.

Along with thinkers in many traditions around the world, such as Buddhism, the ancient Greek thinkers took contingency, change and variability to be a sign of mortality, vulnerability and imperfection. It was factors such as these that gave rise to suffering, war and death. Accordingly, it was thought best if things happen, not randomly and destructively, but because they *should* happen. And they should happen as they do because there is an order of necessity and justice that embraces and encompasses this realm of worldly change. It is not just that things change; it is that a supernatural or transcendent order of justice dictates that they change in the way that they do. It would be too easy and too unsophisticated to think of this order of justice in personal terms, as when we think of it as ordained by a providential God. Rather, fate or destiny was thought of as an impersonal force directed towards order. Everything in the world tends to the way it should be and even when things go wrong, there is natural redress and balance or punishment and reward. This is not unlike the law of karma of which some Eastern religious traditions speak, in which punishments and rewards influence our

117

future lives in a cycle of reincarnation. These beliefs speak of an iron law of destiny that humans cannot escape, and which ensures that the whole cosmos has the moral quality of justice.

While this may sound like a very poetic and somewhat enchanted way of seeing the world, it is remarkable how tenaciously it is held in some form or another even by people in modern times. How often have you heard someone say "That was meant to happen"? Most often such a statement is made about some unlikely event that has proved either fortunate or unfortunate, and the speaker, in uttering it, is accepting it into their lives. Whether or not they consider themselves to be expressing a highly sophisticated metaphysical idea, the implication of the statement is that fate, destiny or some providential, supernatural power has caused this event to happen in a way that is meaningful or beneficial to them. If it was meant to happen, then someone or something meant it to happen. If this someone was not God, then perhaps it was fate or destiny. Either way we cannot but accept it as being for the best. If we see the event as the result of a divine ordinance, of providence, or of a purposeful destiny, we can find some meaning in it that will help us accept it no matter how unfortunate its effects are. When we say that it was meant to happen we don't only mean that it could not have been prevented, but also that what happened is what *should* have happened. Some metaphysical order ensured and required that it should happen and so its happening is good.

The contrasting position would be that the event happened by chance. This might still lead us to accept it. After all, the event happened and nothing can be done to undo its effects. But thinking of it as the result of pure chance does seem to rob the event of any overarching meaning or goodness. Chance is blind and purposeless. To see the event as the result of chance – as a genuine accident – denies us any easy consolation.

Another variation of how these ancient beliefs linger even in modern life is how we often react to bad luck. If we are the victim of a serious illness, or of an accident that causes us an injury, we might say something like "It's just not fair". What we mean by this is not only that it should not have happened, but that it offends against a standard of what we *deserve* to have happen to us. It's not just unfortunate: it's an offence against justice. But against whom or what are we making this complaint? Is there a supernatural power that ensures that only those things happen that should happen, or that everyone gets only what they deserve? Is this unfortunate accident a departure from the proper order of things? Is my injury an offence against the cosmic order of justice? Do I deserve better? Can I claim what I think I deserve from the cosmos itself? It would be irrational to say so, and yet we do. When we are struck down we ask "Why did this happen to me?" as if we thought that there must be a reason or a purpose for everything that happens. But whose purpose would this be? Who or what decides what we deserve from the natural and unpredictable causality of events? We can only hope that these questions have an answer and this hope leads us to believe that they do.

The New Atheists and the validity of faith

That metaphysical beliefs are an expression of deep hopefulness is a point missed by today's so-called "New Atheists". I refer particularly to Richard Dawkins, who argues that belief in God is irrational. He also argues that it is socially harmful and has caused great evils throughout the history of humankind, but I want to focus on the first point. Dawkins argues not only that there is no evidence for the existence of God, but also that all the allegedly rational arguments for his existence do not work. Moreover, all the ways in which God or other supernatural agencies have been used to explain extraordinary events can be shown to be unnecessary, and adequate natural explanations can be put in their place. Dawkins is thinking like the scientist he is. A scientist seeks to explain natural phenomena by positing explanatory hypotheses and then testing them against the facts or against experimental results. Approaching the world in this way leads to the inescapable conclusion that positing God as an explanatory agency is bad science and has no rational warrant. The big bang is a better explanation for the existence of the universe than a highly mysterious creation out of nothing on the part of God. After all, how can he be there when there is nothing? And evolution is a better explanation for the existence of humankind than God's creation of Adam and Eve. Why, if he created us, did he make us such vulnerable, troubled and imperfect beings? Accordingly, Dawkins concludes that belief in a creator God is unnecessary and irrational. In the realm of belief and reason, then, there is no place for metaphysical agencies. In the world constituted by our cognitive faculties there is no need for God.

Dawkins is correct in his argument. If we approach the world and our existence in it in the spirit of science we will not find God. But this discounts the role of hope. I would argue that faith in God is not based on rational argument or evidence. It is not produced by our cognitive faculties. It is produced by hope. In order to make this plausible I need to revisit the distinction between the cognitive faculties and the motivational faculties that I discussed in Chapters 1 and 2. We saw there that many philosophers group our psychological states under the two headings of beliefs and desires, and argue that our beliefs need to be rational and based on evidence while our desires could give expression to our deepest motivations and feelings. This distinction between beliefs and desires allows us to focus on beliefs as purely cognitive states and then to say that there is no evidential or rational ground for belief in God. In their various ways, Socrates, Pascal, Kant, Kierkegaard and Dawkins all agree with this. But they draw different conclusions. Dawkins concludes that there is no God, while Socrates, Pascal, Kant and Kierkegaard respond by turning to our motivational faculties and that species of desire and wish that I have called hope. For them it is not a purely cognitive or scientific question but an emotional and motivational one. They believe in God because they hope, not because they are forced to by empirical evidence or rational proofs.

However, this reintroduces my earlier question. Can this be authentic? Isn't this a case of believing something because you want to even when there is no reason to? Is it a case of self-deception? Is it dishonest? Militant atheists will answer these questions in the affirmative and claim that the hopes of religious believers are motivated by fantasy or desire. Their faith is mere wishful thinking. Belief in God is a delusion created by the fantasy that there is an all-powerful and loving creator who will resolve all of our spiritual anxieties. But the atheists' claim cannot be justified. It is made by someone who does not believe and it emanates from the atheist way of interpreting the world and everything that happens in it. To justify it would require a proof that God does not exist and this would turn the issue into a matter of empirical fact. However, God's being is metaphysical and that means it is beyond our cognitive and rational grasp. There is no scientific, empirical or rational way of deciding either way whether God exists. Accordingly, there is room for a hermeneutical decision as to how one will interpret the world. The atheist chooses to understand the world without a metaphysical dimension, while the believer chooses to understand it with such a dimension. The atheist assumes there is no God and interprets the world accordingly. As a result, he will interpret the faith of religious believers as a delusion. The believer, in the meantime, assumes that God does exist and interprets the world in accordance with that belief. For the believer the atheist is the misguided one. The atheist, in accusing the believer of being delusional and entertaining a fantasy, assumes that the belief in God is false. And the believer, in defending his faith with argument and demonstration, assumes that the atheist's belief is false. But these assumptions cannot be justified either way. The physical and social facts are plain for all to see. The world is the way it is. It is the interpretations that differ.

Take a rainbow. The scientist sees it as the result of light rays refracting off moisture particles. The layman sees it as a thing of beauty. The believer sees it as a promise from God that he will never again punish humanity by drowning. Whatever we make of it, however, the rainbow is what it is. All the rest is interpretation.

Let us use a further example to understand how our hopes influence our interpretations. You may hope and pray that your football team wins a particular match, but if it scores fewer goals than the opposing team it will have lost. No amount of hoping and wishing on your part is going to change that. The game is over and your team lost. It would be irrational and mad to believe that they won just because you hoped so fervently that they would have. This is true, but it is not an entirely apt analogy for religious faith. In this case there is a fact of the matter that we can all apprehend: the score at the end of the match. This is an objective fact that resolves any disagreement and removes any delusion on the issue. But as regards God there is no fact of the matter that we can all apprehend. At the factual and empirical level the world of the believer looks exactly the same as the world of the non-believer. The sun rises and sets, the seasons come and go, people live and die, people help or harm each other, and everything that happens simply happens. It is the way that this is understood and the way it is felt that differs. The believer does not believe something against the evidence in the way that the deluded football fan believes his team won when it is a clear fact that it lost. The believer believes that God exists, has created this world and promises him eternal life by seeing the world in that way. In this way of seeing the world, what happens is seen as an expression of God's providence or even of his miraculous interventions. The believer is making what I called in Chapter 2 a "hermeneutic" claim. The believer interprets the world as a God-created place, history as a God-guided process, and her life as a

God-given opportunity to earn an eternal reward. For his part, the atheist interprets the world as a natural phenomenon, where things simply happen as they do because of the laws of nature or the inclinations of human beings, and where we give those events the most authentic transcendent-but-secular meanings that we can. The facts are not different for either position. It is the ways those facts are interpreted that differ.

The next question, then, is: what drives these various interpretations? Is it reason and empirical evidence or is it hope? My response would be to say that this is a false dichotomy. Believing that life is a God-given opportunity to earn an eternal reward would be an inauthentic and irrational case of believing something just because one wants to, if belief and desire were separate faculties able to influence each other motivationally or causally. Then it would be a case of desire dictating to belief and urging it to be irrational. It would be one part of subjectivity dictating to another part of subjectivity in a way that traditional philosophy would find objectionable. On the traditional view, it should be reason that dictates to desire and hope, rather than the other way round. On this view, the cognitive faculties, of which reason is king, should rule over our emotional and motivational faculties with all their desires, wishes and hopes. But we should think of these faculties differently. Reason and desire are not separate. Belief and hopefulness are not sharply distinct. We are unified beings, not comprising separate faculties that are in conflict with each other, but possessing a unifying integrity. Desire and reason cannot be delineated as separate faculties. Our desire is inextricably bound up with our reason. My notion of subjectivity captures this unity by suggesting that our hidden currents of hopefulness and desire come to expression in our thinking and action. Accordingly, faith and hope cannot be distinguished by attributing them to reason and desire, respectively. They belong together: hopefulness inspires faith and faith inspires hope.

Certainly the delusional football fan would be wrong to believe something only because he wanted it to be true when there is evidence against it. But where there is no clear evidence it is the way we interpret events that matters, and these interpretations can be motivated by our hopefulness. Suppose the umpire awards a free kick to an opposing player for a foul against one of our team. Whatever happened is what happened, but it can be interpreted in various ways. We may interpret it as a bit of staging on the part of the other team while the umpire sees it as a foul committed by our player. This is not a clear empirical judgement as it would be when the umpire judges that the ball is in or out of the field of play. To judge an action to be a foul is to attribute an intention to the offending player. But who can know his intentions besides himself? Accordingly, for the umpire and for the fans, it is a matter of interpretation. If we debated the matter with the umpire we might never agree. It is only because the rules of the game give the umpire the final say in such matters that the game can go on and that a team can lose even as the result of what might seem to be an unfair decision. So far as the rules of the game are concerned, the only thing that matters is the umpire's interpretation. The outrage felt by supporters of the losing team – based as it is on their interpretation of what happened – makes no difference to the outcome. My first point, then, is that an interpretation of the event is a belief that is constructed from what is seen to have happened and also from the biases and hopes of the various observers. The other team's supporters interpret the incident as a foul on the part of our player, we interpret it as a "dive" on the part of their player, and the umpire interprets it as an unlawful interference with the other team's player. There is no impartial or "scientific" court of appeal. Not even a video replay can decide the issue in the way it can decide whether a ball is in or out, because whatever the video shows would still need to be interpreted. My second point is that, in the football example, it is the umpire's authority that decides the issue rather than the facts.

These two points apply to religious beliefs as well. Against Dawkins, I argue that there is no objective and scientific fact of the matter that can decide whether God exists or whether our hopes for an eternal life and religious meanings are sound. Like one's support for a football team, such beliefs are hermeneutic frameworks through which we interpret the world. Unlike the football case, however, we do not have an umpire to decide the issue when we are in dispute. Some people believe in God and others do not. It is not for science or for the spokespersons of the scientific method to decide who is right, and it is not for believers to decide who is right. There is no objectively correct view. There are only the various views that are motivated by the various spiritual anxieties that we all have. Those who hope for eternal life and for religious meaning will tend to believe in God and those who do not harbour such hopes will not. There is neither a fact nor an umpire to decide who is right. And so, from an epistemological point of view, it is quite legitimate to hold metaphysical beliefs such as a belief in God.

There are many other ways in which our hopes and desires legitimately influence our beliefs. We pursue knowledge in those areas that interest us. Today's scientific achievements are driven by curiosity and by the desire for technological progress. Our understanding of our cultures and ways of life is driven by our empathy with others and by our pursuit of meaning in our lives. In much the same way our religious faith is driven by our hope. This is not dishonest because it is not one part of the self deceiving another. It is not desire manipulating belief into adopting an irrational stance. It is a unified and integral stance taken by subjectivity in its comportment towards the world. We see the world through the eyes of our faith and through the rose-coloured glasses of our hopefulness. This is a commitment that can be authentic. As such, being told by Dawkins that there is no rational warrant for such beliefs is beside the point. The truly religious person knows that already. Like Socrates, Pascal, Kant and Kierkegaard, she knows that she does not believe because of evidence, but because seeing the world and her own existence through the eyes of faith can be the most profound expression of her deepest hopes and of her quest for transcendence.

This point allows me now to explain why Aquinas was only partly right when he argued that faith precedes hope. For him, as we saw in the Introduction, we must first believe in God so that this belief can give us grounds to hope for eternal life with him. But this point can be challenged by asking: do we hope because we have faith; or do we have faith because we hope? Aquinas answers the first of these questions in the affirmative when he says that we can hope because we have faith. In contrast, I have argued that we have faith because we hope. Our hope for salvation and for transcendent meanings leads us to believe in a God who can provide them to us.

So how could it be said both that faith inspires hope and that hope inspires faith? There seems to be a dialectical relation between the two. We can make these claims consistent by seeing that this dialectic between hope and faith operates on different levels of consciousness. I argued in Chapter 2 that, in the form of hopefulness, hope is a pre-conscious, pre-intentional aspect of our subjectivity of which we are not normally aware. Our hopefulness is a comportment towards the world that structures the way we see that world. My world is always already a lived environment that is coloured by my hopefulness. Accordingly, I would suggest that it is our hopefulness that inspires faith. However, I am not readily aware that my hopefulness motivates my faith. Consequently, I take my faith to be the primary phenomenon of which I am aware. This is why Aquinas is able to say that my faith comes first and gives me a warrant for hoping for salvation. This is the sequence of psychological states of which I am aware. My point, however, is that beneath the level of my awareness it is an inchoate and pre-conscious form of hopefulness in relation to salvation that motivates me to have that faith. Accordingly, it is my implicit hopefulness that leads to religious faith and this faith, in turn, inspires such explicit meta-physical hopes as my hope for salvation.

An analysis of metaphysical hope

I can now use my ten-point analysis of hope and hopefulness to explicate such metaphysical forms of hope as are illustrated by religious beliefs. As to the first of those ten points, I have already described the spiritual anxieties and needs, and our quest for a meaningful transcendence of everyday life, which constitute our hopefulness. And I have suggested that this hopefulness issues in metaphysical beliefs and religious faith for most of the world's people.

Second, we judge that what we hope for metaphysically is good. It goes without saying that eternal life, the meaningfulness of our lives, the firmness of morality, the intelligibility of the universe, beauty, our sense of identity and belonging, our sense of wholeness, the overcoming of our loneliness and suffering, and the securing of justice will be seen as being of positive value. Of course, people from other traditions and communities may not agree that the specific forms that these values take in our communities are good, and we may not agree that their take on these things are as good as ours, but we will all feel that the solutions that our religion offers to our spiritual anxieties are the best ones. It would seem that conflict can arise from these differences of perspective. And the tragedy is that, in so far as these conflicts rest on differing metaphysical beliefs, and in so far as metaphysical beliefs are not subject to rational appraisal, such conflicts between different traditions may be irresolvable.

Third, metaphysical hope's object is an occurrence that is considered to be possible. Religions tell different stories about their gods, their foundations and their prophets. The details and the names may differ from one religious tradition to another, but the central elements seem to be shared by all of the major faiths around the world. Believers take these stories to be possible, while atheists do not. For believers, the scope of what is possible is wider than it is for those who adopt the secular worldview. Central to religious faith is belief in miracles. Whether it be the parting of the Red Sea to allow the escape of the Hebrews from Egypt, the resurrection of Jesus from the dead, the bodily ascension of Mary into heaven, the night journey (Isra and Mi'raj) of Muhammad to Jerusalem on the wings of an angel, or any of the many miracles ascribed to saints and mythical heroes, the religious believer lives in a world that contains a vastly expanded range of possibilities. Such a believer is therefore able to hope for much more than can a person with a secular outlook.

Fourth, one would expect that metaphysical hope's object would be an occurrence that is considered not to be inevitable. Just as worldly hope is made feasible by the belief that what is hoped for may or may not happen, one would expect that metaphysical hope acknowledges that what it hopes for is not inevitable. However, this does not seem to be true in the context of metaphysical beliefs. I have said that what we hope for is an escape from the fragile, vulnerable, fallible and mortal condition of being human. This hope leads us to seek safety, security, amelioration of the material conditions of life, cognitive certainty, moral rectitude and life after death. But what all this represents is precisely an attempt at escape from contingency. Contingency means that nothing is predetermined. Nothing is fated or preordained. Nothing is immune to change or transformation. Nothing can be absolutely depended on, not even the promises of a God. But these contingencies of life are what metaphysical hope seeks to overcome. In Chapter 1 I argued that we can be genuine in our hope for things only if we take those things not to be inevitable. John would not hope that it would not rain if he thought either that rain was inevitable or that it was completely impossible. He can hope for it not to rain because he knows that the occurrence of rain is contingent: it might or it might not happen. But when we move to the realm of metaphysics, we are talking about hopes that have a greater dimension of ultimacy. What we long for is certainty and absoluteness. We want assurance and guarantees. We cannot abide the thought that things might happen by chance. Perhaps it is because the world as we know it cannot offer us such certainty and such guarantees that our hope leads us to believe in a metaphysical realm of reality in which all contingency is overcome.

This is another example of the dialectical relation between hope and faith that I mentioned in connection with Aquinas. Our explicit hope is for things that we take to be contingent. But our deeper and less conscious hopefulness is that things not be contingent. This deeper hopefulness gives rise to faith in truths and realities that are indubitable, universal, certain and eternal. This faith is, then, an attempt to overcome the uncertainties and fallibilities of actual human life by appealing to absolute realities in which all contingency is overcome. The real world is full of contingencies. And so we conceive of a metaphysical world in which those contingencies are replaced by the unquestionable will of the gods or of fate and destiny. We crave a world in which what happens is what was meant to happen.

Fifth, metaphysical hope is directed towards the future as conceived by the person who hopes. Once again, this point has been implicitly covered already. The point to add is that, at the metaphysical level, our hope is that our future is unlimited. We want to be immortal. At one level this is a fantasy, but at another it is a perfectly natural sentiment. Most people do not want to die. The songs of slaves that Obama referred to in his speech include hymns about "crossing Jordan" or going to the promised land. They express a belief in a blissful life ahead, in which our sufferings will be left behind and we will meet our deceased loved ones again in heaven. All the metaphysical entities that we conjure into being

129

with our imagination and with our interpretations of worldly events speak to us of a glorious future: life after death, angels to lead us to the heavenly gates, God with his indubitable promise of eternal reward, even hell, that ultimate and inescapable punishment for those who are evil. Many religious traditions speak of a last judgement in which God will separate the sheep from the goats and reward the former with eternal bliss. These events are all envisaged as existing in our futures and in a realm different from our current existence in this vale of tears. Even Buddhism, which does not believe in God as a supernatural person, includes some traditions that believe in a future salvation for all. These traditions speak of a "Maitreya Buddha", who will come to teach us all enlightenment in a distant future.

Messianism, millenarianism and belief in a second coming are further expressions of this future-orientation of metaphysical hope. There are many who believe that their god will return to this world in order to usher in a new time of glory and peace in which all conflicts will be resolved. And it is not only the major world religions that propagate such beliefs. The Manseren cult, or Koreri movement, which flared up from time to time over many years on the island of Biak-Numfor on the northern coast of West Papua was centred on belief in an ancestor called Manseren Mangundi, whose birth was magical and who taught his people their traditional ways. However, he was disappointed in them and was said to have departed to the west whence he would return when the time was right. Every now and then, the people of Biak are stirred by prophets or *konors* to believe that the time is indeed right and that they should burn their houses and crops and kill their pigs in anticipation of the great gifts of cargo and food that Manseren will bring on his return. When the Christian missionaries came, this legend was assimilated with the story of Jesus and the promise of his return after the apocalypse. Moreover, just as *konors* were believed to be able to heal the sick and protect their people from sorcery, so

Jesus was accepted as an oracle and healer of great magical power. During the Second World War, prophets mixed all these magical and messianic beliefs together to encourage the people to rise up against the Dutch and then the Japanese in order to reaffirm their traditional customs, restore their ancient beliefs and usher in the return of Manseren. Such prophets taught that their oppressors' bullets would turn to water and that their own spears would turn into rifles on the appointed day. As a result some five hundred of their followers were gunned down by the Japanese.

Nor were such beliefs unique to West Papua. In the Fifth Xhosa War of 1819 in South Africa, a prophet arose named Makana, who promised his Xhosa tribal followers that the British bullets fired against them would turn to water. The cult of Jon Frum on the island of Tanna, in what is today Vanuatu, is but one of many cargo cults that exist in the Pacific, which hope for magical gifts of goods and wealth that the indigenous peoples have seen arriving from overseas for the Europeans. It is frequently believed that this cargo comes from the power of the Bible and that the missionaries have not given indigenous peoples all of the information that the Bible contains in order to withhold the cargo from them. For many years, adherents of the Jon Frum cult built airstrips and wooden towers in imitation of American practices during the war in order to allow the cargo to arrive. They even destroyed their own goods so as to make way for the wealth that they believed would come to them if they lived in the ways their indigenous prophets preached.

The role that hope plays in these beliefs and practices will be obvious. Their orientation is clearly towards the future, a future that is more a construction of hope and faith than it is a prediction based on a sound understanding of the present. These beliefs may be rational within the worldview of these traditional communities but, objectively, the futures that they envisage remain unattainable. Given that these communities were subject to disruption of their ways of life owing to colonialism and the new belief systems preached by missionaries, and given that they can see the power and affluence of their oppressors, the beliefs that their hopes for a better life inspire will seem rational to them. The tragedies that their hopes can lead to could be avoided only by adopting an objective stance that is uninfluenced by the hopes that these communities reasonably entertain. But if desire and reason together create a unified worldview – if hopefulness inspires faith – then members of these communities could not readily access a separate, objective, critical faculty of reason with which to evaluate their beliefs.

Seventh, metaphysical hope is directed at circumstances over which the person hoping does not have complete control. The believer hopes for the blessings of heaven and for eternal salvation. Clearly, these are not matters over which the believer can exercise control. It is part of what defines a god that he or she cannot be controlled by human beings. Indeed, many theologians warn us against the presumption of thinking that we can influence the gods to intervene in our lives through our rituals, sacrifices and prayers. Nevertheless, there are many believers who do not heed this warning. As I noted in Chapter 1, prayer is often seen as an attempt to secure favours and help from a god who must then be believed to be concerned for us in such mundane ways. If we thought we could get what we wanted from the gods just be asking for it, there would be no need to hope for those benefits. We could just secure them by engaging in the appropriate ritual of supplication. As Aquinas reminds us, however, salvation is difficult and arduous to obtain. It is for this reason that we must hope for it even as we work towards it.

Eighth, metaphysical hope ought to lead to appropriate action when such action is available on the part of the person who hopes. So far as the religious forms of metaphysical hope are concerned, this leads us to commit ourselves to the many practices, rituals and observances that religion ordains. Whether it is dietary laws, codes of dress, attendance at church or the mosque, the giving of alms or the observance of holy days, religion is as much about practice as it is about belief. This point is missed by those critics of religion who lampoon Jewish and Muslim prohibitions against eating pork, for example, on the grounds that any beliefs about health and diet on which such rules are based are primitive and unscientific. As I have already suggested, this prohibition is not imposed for the sake of health and diet. Its purpose is the felt need to express one's religious hope and faith and affirm one's identity. Once one is a member of a particular religious tradition, the rules laid down by that tradition are to be followed so that one can reasonably hope for the metaphysical rewards that that tradition offers and so that one can identify oneself with that tradition. It is quite arbitrary what such rules might be. For Hindus it is not eating beef, for Jews and Muslims it is not eating pork, for Catholics it is fasting in Lent, and so on. There is no worldly or scientific rationale for any of these rules, although there might be sociological explanations for how they came about. They are simply a way of demonstrating a devotee's membership and of legitimizing the hopes that adherents can then have for their salvation. No such hope would be genuine if one were not prepared to do something towards achieving it. But in so far as the hope is metaphysical, there is nothing of a purely worldly or rational nature that one can do to merit its fulfilment.

Ninth, metaphysical hope has the psychological structure of supplication. This point is the key to everything that has been said so far. We hope for an alleviation of the burdens of the human condition and so we appeal to a metaphysical power to save us. Our hope is a supplication. It then moves on to create an interpretative framework that allows us to see the whole of human reality through rose-coloured glasses, in which the rose colouring is created by religious belief. This then presents us with a world that contains just those meanings and reassurances which answer to our spiritual anxieties and metaphysical supplications.

Last, and tenth, metaphysical hope ought to be rational and realistic. We can see from everything that has been said so far that there is now considerable pressure on seeing what could be meant by "rational and realistic" in the context of metaphysical hope. Dawkins doesn't see any of it as rational and realistic. But his definition of what this means is set by the scientific worldview and its methods of enquiry. Will this worldview serve us here? Scientific rationality is immensely valuable in the realm of worldly concerns, but it may not be appropriate in the realm of metaphysical hope. As we noted with reference to the sometimes bizarre beliefs of colonized peoples, hope generates beliefs that can seem rational to those who hold them even when they are mortally dangerous. For a Jewish or Muslim religious believer it makes perfect sense to shun pork. For religious believers more generally it makes perfect sense to believe in gods, angels and souls. Theology is the academic discipline whose task it is to make sense of these things. Despite the many contradictions and absurdities that religious dogmas seem to present to non-believers, theologians are able to make them coherent and plausible. Of course, this only works within the framework of an interpretation of reality that sees it as god-created, that sees human life as god-directed and that believes that miracles are possible. Once such assumptions are made, intellectual skill will meet no obstacles in creating a coherent creed. In this way religious hope can indeed be made to seem rational and realistic to those for whom hopefulness has generated faith.

Conclusion

The question that this analysis of religion as an expression of metaphysical hope raises is not whether religion is true, rationally justifiable from an objective point of view or realistic. I shall not ask the questions that the New Atheists have raised. Rather, I shall raise a new question: is the religious expression of metaphysical hope a humanly valuable or worthwhile response to the fragile, vulnerable, fallible and mortal condition of being human? Socrates claimed that the risk of believing was a noble one. But is it? We have seen that the differing metaphysical beliefs of various religious traditions can lead to conflict between them. They can also lead individuals to presumption and a life of fantasy. So can our hopes for transcendence be fulfilled by non-metaphysical objects? Are the world itself and the human beings who live in it sufficiently valuable in themselves to be, for us, a source of consolation in the face of death, meaningfulness in our lives, adherence to morality, experiences of understanding and beauty, a sense of identity and belonging, feelings of wholeness, acceptance and solidarity, and the institutions of justice that we all hope for? My hope is that they are.

Epilogue: the virtue of hope

Throughout this book, I have used Aristotle's framework for understanding virtues to make two suggestions. The first was that hope represented a set of attitudes, emotions and motivations that lay in a median position between forms of excess and forms of deficiency. The extremes that virtuous hope avoids are the excesses of presumption and the deficiencies of despair and resignation, while the non-virtuous extremes of hopefulness were naivety and fantasy at the excessive end of the spectrum, and cynicism at the deficient end. People will fail to display the virtue of hope if they lack the confidence and hopefulness to embark on projects whose success cannot be guaranteed. This would be resignation and, in even more acute cases, despair. And people will fail to display the virtue of hopefulness if they lack the conviction that their projects are worth the effort and risk involved in being committed to them. The forms of excess are somewhat more various and complex. We have seen that one form of excess of hope is presumption, which involves hoping for more than is possible, expecting others to provide it, and making no commitment to the action that hope requires. Similarly, the person who is excessive in the sphere of hopefulness trusts in others and expects good things in the future to a naive degree. Such a person neither sees risks nor anticipates problems. The line between such excessive optimism and living a life of fantasy could not be easily drawn.

But having explored hope and hopefulness in the domains of the clinic, of politics and of religion, I would now suggest that a further form of excess is an excess of supplication. This is the frame of mind in which a person places so much trust in natural forces, powerful people or metaphysical agencies that they relinquish responsibility for their own actions and their rational grasp of reality. Presumption, fantasy and the excesses of supplication would lead us to think that the universe owes us our well-being; that we have a claim on fate; that we deserve the good or ill that befalls us; and that the gods or their agents should guarantee justice to us. We have seen that the problematic sides of hope and hopefulness stem from such forms of excessive supplication. Harvey Nuland appeals to his brother and relinquishes responsibility for his treatment decisions to him. As a result he is encouraged to hope against hope and his suffering is needlessly extended. In the political sphere, the element of supplication can lead ordinary citizens to place excessive trust in charismatic political leaders who promise to realize their hopes. It can even facilitate the emergence of demagogues and tyrants. Ideological dreams of social progress can cross over into the sphere of metaphysical hope and encourage expectations of messianic deliverance from troubled times, or apocalyptic changes in which cosmic powers deliver the chosen ones from perdition. A second coming of the saviour or the restoration of a global caliphate would be the ultimate response to the supplication and hopes of a suffering people. The element of supplication is most clearly present in religion and other forms of metaphysical hope in that these are centred on supernatural beings that are believed to be able to deliver us from evil and assure us of our eternal salvation. For hope to become virtuous, therefore, it must overcome any excess of supplication that is inherent in it.

The virtue of hope involves seeing the world as it is, without presumption, naivety, fantasy or despair. In such a world, things happen because they are caused to rather than because of some metaphysical purpose or destiny. Sometimes they happen to me and sometimes they happen to other people. Sometimes they are to my benefit and sometimes they are not. That is just the way things are in this changeable world in which chance has as much of a role as predictable causality. Admittedly, I have some control over my life in that I can plan what I will do next and reduce the risks to my well-being. And I can ask others to help me. But my control is never complete. I cannot guarantee that my plans will come to fruition. The laws of nature are what they are and things just happen because of them. The virtue of hope acknowledges this and interprets the universe as indifferent to our needs. It refuses to wear any excessively rose-coloured metaphysical glasses. It sees that hardship, injury, deprivation and even death are simply what happens as a result of the laws of physics and biology. And if what happens is that I find myself in a situation in which I am starving, for example, then, from the point of view of the universe that is just bad luck. I do not have a claim on justice simply because I have an extreme need or an intense hope. I might have a claim against my fellow human beings and the institutions that they have set up, but I have no basis for a claim against the universe or the gods. It is not virtuous to make a claim on heaven when things go badly for us.

Aristotle's schema would lead us to expect there to be a deficient degree of supplication in the sphere of hope as well. One could imagine a person who never asks anyone for help and thinks that they can fulfil their hopes entirely on their own. Such a person would seek to be self-sufficient in all their projects and fail to see opportunities for cooperation and solidarity with others. They would lack reasons for entering into relationships with others and would be deficient in sociability and perhaps even friendship. Hope is one of the many bonds that secure our attachment to others. Family bonds, sociability and political solidarity are forged by the mutuality that the element of supplication in hope produces. And I might add that if those attachments fulfil our needs and respond to our anxieties, there will be no need to project them into the metaphysical realm so as to direct our supplication onto supernatural beings.

My second Aristotelian suggestion was that to be a virtue, a character trait or a state of mind must be directed upon a noble goal. In the case of hope the most general form of this goal was that of living well, with and for others, in a just world. Perhaps living this way would resolve the spiritual anxieties that I described in Chapter 5. Certainly Aristotle's claim was that living this way would make us happy. Pursuing this goal will help us to entertain authentic hopes that can be rational, realistic and directed towards future goals that we will judge to be good. But does this mean that we cannot be happy unless we achieve a life that is totally fulfilled, relationships that are deep, lasting and without disappointments, and a global society in which no injustice could ever occur? No, not only are such grand goals unattainable, but in a multicultural world there will be disagreements as to what they could mean in concrete terms. Even our own reflection will often fail to yield a precise understanding of what those goals require of us. Uncertainty and contingency are endemic in the human condition. We cannot be given any guarantees. Our actions are faulty, fallible and fragile. Nevertheless, we must continue to hope that we can live well, with and for others, in a just world. Appropriate and committed action towards such goals will make them more attainable than we might have thought, and attainable enough for our happiness.

Further reading

Introduction

For a general discussion of the role of virtue in ethics see my *Understanding Virtue Ethics* (2006). Aristotle's views on the virtues are developed in his *Nicomachean Ethics*, of which there are many editions and translations.

Thomas Aquinas's discussion of the emotion of hope is to be found in his *Summa Theologica*: "First Part of the Second Part", question 23, "How the passions differ from one another", and question 40, "The irascible passions, and first, of hope and despair". He develops his understanding of what theological hope is in his *Summa Theologica*: "Second Part of the Second Part", question 17, "Hope, considered in itself".

The virtues as conceived by positive psychology are expounded in Christopher Peterson and Martin E. P. Seligman's *Character Strengths and Virtues: A Handbook and Classification* (2004).

1. Defining hope

For a discussion of hope as linked to action see Patrick Shade's *Habits of Hope* (2001). Because Shade links hope strongly to action he discusses virtues relevant to action in the face of difficulty, such as persistence, resourcefulness and courage.

Joseph Pieper's *On Hope* (1986) explores the topic purely from a Christian religious perspective. A very scholarly and thorough treatment of hope can be found in Joseph J. Godfrey's *The Philosophy of Human Hope* (1987). Godfrey discusses the theories of Ernst Bloch, Gabriel Marcel and Immanuel Kant, and directs his discussion towards "ultimate hope" in God. Gabriel Marcel's views can be found in his *Homo Viator* (1951). Marcel approaches hope from a phenomenological and existential perspective and includes discussions of Heidegger and Nietzsche. Like so many writers on hope, he leads his readers to religious concepts of absoluteness and ultimacy in the objects of our hopes.

2. Being hopeful

For a discussion of the "ethical aim" that is said to inform all of our lives see, Paul Ricoeur's *Oneself as Another* (1992).

3. Hope in the clinic

Several articles on hope in the clinic from both nursing and medical perspectives can be found in *Interdisciplinary Perspectives on Hope*, edited by Jaklin A. Eliott (2005), and see especially Kaye Herth's "State of the Science of Hope in Nursing Practice" (2005), which quotes Madelein Vaillot's article "Hope: The Restoration of Being" (1970), focusing nursing research on to the topic of hope. I also drew some ideas for this chapter from Mary Crookshank and Eric J. Cassell's "The Place of Hope in Clinical Medicine" (2005).

Martin Heidegger has made much of how time structures our existence toward our deaths in *Being and Time* (1962). For a more accessible discussion of the existential dimensions of death see Todd May's *Death* (2009). For a discussion of technological brinkmanship in the clinic see Chapter 8, "Accepting Death", in my *Life, Death and Subjectivity* (2004). For a compelling account of the needs and anxieties that accompany illness see Havi Carel's *Illness* (2008).

4. Hope and politics

Barack Obama's keynote speech at the Democratic Convention of 2004 can be found at, www.barackobama.com/2004/07/27/keynote_address_at_the_2004_de.php (accessed February 2011). Although hope is not discussed in it as such, Obama's famous phrase has become the title of his book, *The Audacity of Hope* (2006). Thomas Hobbes's myth of the origins of politics can be found in his book, *Leviathan, or The Matter, Forme and Power of a Common Wealth Ecclesiasticall and Civil* (1651), which is available in many editions.

Another interesting discussion of hope as a socially shared outlook on life and on politics in different cultures is found in Dominique Moïsi's *The Geopolitics of Emotion* (2009). For a discussion of what happens when a whole society has hope taken from it because of conquest, see Jonathan Lear's *Radical Hope* (2007). Social and political hope in the face of the danger of nuclear war is advocated by Karl Jaspers in *The Future of Mankind* (1961). A further enquiry into hope as a political motivation is found in Mary Zournazi's *Hope* (2002), which consists in a number of extended interviews with writers, activists and political philosophers. Ernst Bloch's *The Principle of Hope* (1995) is a very thorough discussion with a focus on politics, in which it is argued that only a socialist society can realize our hopes for the improvement of human life. I also drew some ideas for this chapter from Bernard P. Dauenhauer's *The Politics of Hope* (1986). Judith Shklar, in her "The Liberalism of Fear" (1989), highlights the quandary of modern politics as polarized between the quest for freedom and the fear of oppression.

The theory that we are all evolving to a glorious "omega point" is developed in Teilhard de Chardin's *The Phenomenon of Man* (1959). This view is criticized by Josef Pieper in *Hope and History* (1969), but then Pieper himself goes on to posit a metaphysical hope which reaches beyond our deaths.

For a thorough discussion of the history of the idea of progress as stemming from the Enlightenment, see Sidney Pollard's *The Idea of Progress* (1968). For a historical account of the political struggles to ban the slave trade see Adam Hochschild's *Bury the Chains* (2005). A truly pessimistic discussion of how the ideas of progress and our faith in the Enlightenment has led us astray is provided in John

Gray's *Al Qaeda and What It Means to be Modern* (2003). For an elaboration of the global scale of our political and moral responsibilities, see my *Cosmopolitanism* (2009).

For an excellent discussion of utopian, messianic and millenarian movements see, Alfred Braunthal's *Salvation and the Perfect Society* (1979). Braunthal does not confine himself to the Western tradition but traces the development of such views in Asian and Middle Eastern traditions as well. The dangers of too much hope in the social and political domains are eloquently discussed by Barbara Ehrenreich in her *Smile or Die* (2010). Another sceptic about hope, especially in the context of political rhetoric (and about political issues such as global warming) is Roger Scruton in his *The Uses of Pessimism and the Danger of False Hope* (2010).

5. Hope and religion

The statistics on religious adherents were found at www.adherents.com/Religions_By_Adherents.html (accessed February 2011). My account of our spiritual needs is consistent with the account of human needs given by Abraham Maslow in his "A Theory of Human Motivation" (1943), and more fully developed in his book *Motivation and Personality* (1954). For a profound exploration of the fragile, vulnerable, fallible and mortal condition of being human, see Paul Ricoeur's *Fallible Man* (1986). For a very thorough and scientific treatment of hope that gives full recognition to its spiritual and religious dimensions, see Anthony Scioli and Henry Biller's *Hope in the Age of Anxiety* (2009). Albert Camus discusses the myth of Sisyphus in his *The Myth of Sisyphus and Other Essays* (1955).

For "Pascal's Wager", see Blaise Pascal's *Pensées* (1966), § 418. (Some commentators ascribe the argument to §233, but this number precedes a reordering of the text by French editors and appears only in older editions.) Kant suggests that our hope for moral justice in the form of eternal rewards and punishments can justify belief in God in his *Religion Within the Limits of Reason Alone* (1960). Søren Kierkegaard expounds his views on faith being based in subjectivity in a number of texts but most notably in *Concluding Unscientific Postscript* (1941).

The most notable of the "New Atheist" books is Richard Dawkins's *The God Delusion* (2006). Christopher Hitchens lampoons the prohibition on eating pork in his *God is not Great* (2007), chapter 3.

My description of the Manseren cult, of Makana in South Africa and of the cargo cults in the Pacific were sourced from Bryan Wilson's exhaustive study of religious cult movements in traditional societies impacted by colonial exploitation and missionary activity, entitled *Magic and the Millennium* (1973). See also Marvin Harris's *Cows, Pigs, Wars and Witches* (1975) for truly amazing stories about cargo cults as a form of messianism, and other expressions of hope gone mad. You can read about one Yehuda Glick, a forty-four-year-old US-born Jew who is executive director of the Temple Institute in Jerusalem, which is preparing for the arrival of the Messiah by seeking to build the third temple and has already acquired golden worship vestments and objects, on www.templeinstitute.org/main.htm (accessed February 2011). Ancient Greek conceptions of the world are very eloquently described by F. M. Cornford in his *Before and After Socrates* (1932).

There is a profound exploration of our spiritual anxieties in, Charles Taylor's *A Secular Age* (2007). For an account of how our spiritual anxieties might be resolved in a non-religious framework, see J. Heath Atchley's *Encountering the Secular* (2009).

Epilogue

The idea that hope should be realistic rather than utopian is discussed at length, with reference to such writers as Schopenhauer, Nietzsche, Cervantes and Camus, in Joshua Foa Dienstag's *Pessimism* (2006).

Bibliography

Aquinas, T. *Summa Theologica*, www.newadvent.org/summa (accessed February 2011).

Aristotle. *Nicomachean Ethics*, http://classics.mit.edu/Aristotle/nicomachaen.html (accessed February 2011).

Atchley, J. H. 2009. *Encountering the Secular: Philosophical Endeavors in Religion and Culture*. Charlottesville, VA: University of Virginia Press.

Bloch, E. 1995. *The Principle of Hope*, N. Plaice, S. Plaice & P. Knight (trans.). Cambridge, MA: MIT Press.

Braunthal, A. 1979. *Salvation and the Perfect Society: The Eternal Quest*. Amherst, MA: University of Massachusetts Press.

Brookshank, M. A. & E. J. Cassell 2005. "The Place of Hope in Clinical Medicine". In *Interdisciplinary Perspectives on Hope*, J. A. Eliott (ed.), 231–9. New York: Nova Science.

Camus, A. 1955. *The Myth of Sisyphus and Other Essays*, J. O'Brien (trans.). Harmondsworth: Penguin.

Carel, H. 2008. *Illness*. Stocksfield: Acumen.

Cornford, F. M. 1932. *Before and After Socrates*. Cambridge: Cambridge University Press.

Dawkins, R. 2006. *The God Delusion*. London: Transworld.

Dauenhauer, B. P. 1986. *The Politics of Hope*. London: Routledge & Kegan Paul.

de Chardin, T. 1959. *The Phenomenon of Man*, B. Wall (trans.). London: Collins.

Dienstag, J. F. 2006. *Pessimism: Philosophy, Ethic, Spirit*. Princeton, NJ: Princeton University Press.

Ehrenreich, B. 2010. *Smile or Die: How Positive Thinking Fooled America and the World*. London: Granta. Originally published as *Bright-Sided: How the Relentless Promotion of Positive Thinking Has Undermined America* (New York: Henry Holt, 2009).

Eliott, J. A. (ed.) 2005. *Interdisciplinary Perspectives on Hope*. New York: Nova Science.

Geach, P. 1977. *The Virtues*. Oxford: Oxford University Press.

Gray, J. 2003. *Al Qaeda and What It Means to be Modern*. London: Faber.

Godfrey, J. J. 1987. *The Philosophy of Human Hope*. Dordrecht: Martinus Nijhoff.

Harris, M. 1975. *Cows, Pigs, Wars and Witches: The Riddles of Culture*. London: Hutchinson.

Heidegger, M. 1962. *Being and Time*, J. Macquarrie & E. Robinson (trans.). New York: Harper & Row.

Herth, K. 2005. "State of the Science of Hope in Nursing Practice: Hope, the Nurse, and the Patient". In *Interdisciplinary Perspectives on Hope*, J. A. Eliott (ed.), 169–211. New York: Nova Science.

Hitchens, C. 2007. *God is not Great: How Religion Poisons Everything*. New York: Hachette.

Hobbes, T. 1651. *Leviathan, or The Matter, Forme and Power of a Common Wealth Ecclesiasticall and Civil*. www.gutenberg.org/etext/3207 (accessed February 2011).

Hochschild, A. 2005. *Bury the Chains: Prophets and Rebels in the Fight to Free an Empire's Slaves*. Boston, MA: Houghton Mifflin.

Jaspers, K. 1961. *The Future of Mankind*, E. B. Ashton (trans.). Chicago, IL: University of Chicago Press.

Kant, I. 1781. *The Critique of Pure Reason*, http://ebooks.adelaide.edu.au/k/kant/immanuel/k16p/index.html (accessed January 2011).

Kant, I. 1960. *Religion Within the Limits of Reason Alone*, T. M. Greene & H. H. Hudson (trans.). New York: Harper & Row.

Kierkegaard, S. 1941. *Concluding Unscientific Postscript*, D. F. Swenson (trans.), W. Lowrie (intro. and notes). Princeton, NJ: Princeton University Press.

Lear, J. 2007. *Radical Hope: Ethics in the Face of Cultural Devastation*, Cambridge, MA: Harvard University Press.

Marcel, G. 1951. *Homo Viator: Introduction to a Metaphysic of Hope*, E. Craufurd (trans.). Chicago, IL: Henry Regnery.

Marcel, G. 1995. *The Philosophy of Existentialism*, M. Harari (trans.). New York: Carol Publishing.

Maslow, A. 1943. "A Theory of Human Motivation". *Psychological* Review **50**(4): 370–96.

Maslow, A. 1954. *Motivation and Personality*. New York: Harper & Row.

May, T. 2009. *Death*. Stocksfield: Acumen.

Moïsi, D. 2009. *The Geopolitics of Emotion: How Cultures of Fear, Humiliation, and Hope are Reshaping the World*. New York: Doubleday.

Nuland, S. B. 1993. *How We Die*. New York: Random House.

Obama, B. 2006. *The Audacity of Hope: Thoughts on Reclaiming the American Dream*. New York: Random House.

Pascal, B. 1966. *Pensées*, A. J. Krailsheimer (trans.). Harmondsworth: Penguin.

Peterson, C. & M. E. P. Seligman, 2004. *Character Strengths and Virtues: A Handbook and Classification*. New York: Oxford University Press/American Psychological Association.

Pieper, J. 1969. *Hope and History*, R. Winston & C. Winston (trans.). London: Burns & Oates.

Pieper, J. 1986. *On Hope*. San Francisco, CA: Ignatius Press.

Plato, 1954. *Phaedo*, H. Tredennick (trans.). Harmondsworth: Penguin.

Pollard, S. 1968. *The Idea of Progress: History and Society*. Harmondsworth: Penguin.

Ricoeur, P. 1986. *Fallible Man*, C. A. Kelbley (rev. trans.). New York: Fordham University Press.

Ricoeur, P. 1992. *Oneself as Another*, K. Blamey (trans.). Chicago, IL: University of Chicago Press.

Scioli, A. & H. Biller 2009. *Hope in the Age of Anxiety*. Oxford: Oxford University Press.

Scruton, R. 2010. *The Uses of Pessimism and the Danger of False Hope*. London: Atlantic.

Shade, P. 2001. *Habits of Hope: A Pragmatic Theory.* Nashville, TN: Vanderbilt University Press.

Shklar, J. 1989. "The Liberalism of Fear". In *Liberalism and the Moral Life*, N. Rosenblum (ed.), 21–39. Cambridge, MA: Harvard University Press.

Taylor, C. 2007. *A Secular Age.* Cambridge, MA: Harvard University Press.

Vaillot, M. 1970. "Hope: The Restoration of Being". *American Journal of Nursing* **70**(2): 268–73.

van Hooft, S. 2004. *Life, Death and Subjectivity: Moral Sources in Bioethics.* New York: Rodopi.

van Hooft, S. 2006. *Understanding Virtue Ethics.* Chesham: Acumen.

van Hooft, S. 2009. *Cosmopolitanism: A Philosophy for Global Ethics.* Stocksfield: Acumen.

Wilson, B. 1973. *Magic and the Millennium.* London: Heinemann.

Zournazi, M. 2002. *Hope: New Philosophies for Change.* Annandale, NSW: Pluto Press.

Index

alternative medicine 115
anger 20, 41, 56, 62
anxieties 37, 65, 67, 84; *see also*
   clinical anxieties, political
   anxieties, spiritual anxieties
anxiety, as a condition for hope
   12–13, 21–3, 31, 46, 64–5, 76
apocalypse 130, 137
apocalyptic visions 99
Aquinas, Thomas 4–7, 29–30, 32, 35,
   56, 58, 126, 129, 132
Aristotle 44–7, 55–6, 62, 82, 136, 139
Armageddon 100
attachment 138
audacity of hope 82
Australia 93
authenticity of belief 111, 121–5
autonomy 72

beauty 104, 114, 122, 127, 135
bioethics 71–3
Bolsheviks 99
Buddhism 117, 130

Camus, Albert 103–4
capitalism 90–91
cargo cult 130–31
Catholic rituals 115–16, 133
chance 106, 118, 129, 138
Changeling 26
character strengths 8
Christianity 38, 61, 102, 110, 113
Christian missionaries 130
clinical anxieties 67–9
cognitive faculties 120–21
Collins, Christine 26–9, 33, 35–6,
   42–3

conflict between religions 127
contingency 14, 17, 32, 39, 88, 91–2,
   117, 128–9, 139
cooperation 84, 138
courage 1, 3
cynicism 63–4, 82–3, 87, 134

Dawkins, Richard 119–20, 125, 134
death 66, 69–73, 103, 138
   acceptance of 73–4
   denial of 73, 75
   fear of 68, 70, 76–7
   peaceful 77–9
delusion, belief in God as 121
democracy 92, 99
depression 45
Descartes, René 113
despair 5, 45, 94, 111, 136–7
destiny 88, 91, 99–100, 112, 117,
   129, 137
devil 61
dialectic between hope and faith
   126, 129; *see also* faith based on
   hope

Enlightenment 89–91
ethical aim 57–9
eternal life 8, 70–71, 107–9
   belief in 111; *see also* life after
   death
ethical values 2, 5–6, 10
evil 58–62
evolution 91, 120

faith 7, 37, 63, 107–19, 111–12,
   120–26
   based on hope 126, 129

fantasy 40, 46, 63, 121, 135, 137
fate 32, 37, 87, 92, 117–18, 128–9, 137
fear 5, 23, 58, 69, 84
Fifth Xhosa War 131
freedom 84, 88, 106
French Revolution 99
Freud, Sigmund 54
Frum, Jon 131
fundamentalism 85

Galileo 113
Geach, Peter 38
globalization 86–7
God 6–7, 37, 45, 61, 63, 100, 107, 130–32
existence of 109–14, 119–23
government, role of 39, 84–6
grace 116

happiness 2, 7–8, 55–7, 59, 64, 78, 139
healing 105, 115
hermeneutics 60–61, 121–2, 125
Hinduism 102, 114, 133
history and politics 59, 89, 122
goal of 90–92, 98
Hitler, Adolf 96
Hobbes, Thomas 83
hope defined 46
admits of degrees 21
against hope 42, 73, 137
authentic and inauthentic 33–5, 45–7, 139
beliefs and desires combined in 52–4, 120–23
Christian 38
cognitive dimensions of 40–42, 52, 63
contrasted with wishes 20–23
as an emotion 43
intentionality of 48
episodic 48–50
ethical significance of 39–40
nobility of 42, 51, 108, 117, 135, 139
rationality of 40–43
relation to faith 126–29
as a spur to action 4, 9, 25–35
as a virtue 40

hopefulness 49–51
contrasted with hope 52
as deep structure 64
human fallibility 61, 113

identity 10, 85, 92, 105, 114–15, 127, 133–5
illness 45, 66–8
and justice 119
as a spiritual issue 115
injury 66
intellectual virtue 3–4, 44
intentions 18, 31–2, 56, 124
interpretation 122–4, 134; see also hermeneutics
Islam 100, 102, 114, 133

Jesus 110, 115, 116, 128, 130, 131
Joy 4, 51, 63
joyfulness 52, 65
Judaism 100, 114, 133–4
justice 8, 64, 88, 91, 106, 110, 116, 138
as object of hope 117–19, 58

Kant, Immanuel 7–8, 41, 56, 110, 113, 120, 125
Kelly, Gene 12
Kierkegaard, Søren 110–11, 120, 125
knowledge, the pursuit of 104

law of karma 112, 117
life after death 8, 70–71, 107, 111, 128, 130; see also eternal life
loneliness 106, 116
Lourdes 72, 115
love 4, 5, 51–2, 54, 57–8, 106, 116
of wisdom 109
luck 3, 9, 14, 32, 38, 91, 118, 138; see also chance

Maitreya Buddha 130
Makana 131
Manseren cult 130–31
Marcel, Gabriel 37, 44
meaninglessness 104, 112
medical technology 73–4
messianism 95, 99–100, 112, 130, 137

metaphysical hope   107–9, 112, 127–34
metaphysics   107, 113, 129
millenarianism   100, 112, 130
miracle   72, 75, 77, 79, 128
Muhammad   128
morality   8, 59, 110, 104, 112, 127
moral law   110, 113
Moses   112
motivational states   4, 9, 41, 52, 68, 120–21, 123

naivety   62–3, 136–7
neoliberalism   85
New Atheists   119, 134
Nietzsche, Friedrich   51
nirvana   71
Nuland, Sherwin B.   73

Obama, Barack   81–2, 87, 92–6, 101, 107, 129
objectivity   11, 17, 74, 112–13, 122, 125, 131–2
omega point   91
optimism   9, 49, 62, 82, 136
original sin   61

palliative care   66
Pascal, Blaise   109–10, 120, 125
paternalism   71
pessimism   9, 52, 63
Peterson, Christopher   8–9
planning   9, 32
Plato   41, 113
political anxieties   83–5
political participation   94–5
political vision   98
politics   81–3, 93–4
pork, prohibition of   114, 133–4
positive psychology   8
prayer   35–9, 132
presumption   44–5, 63, 73, 87, 93, 132, 135, 137
private sphere   85–6
progress, the idea of   88–92
providence   107, 118, 122
prudence   4
psychology   51
public discourse   95

pyramids of Egypt   114

Rapture, the   100
rationality   3, 43, 110, 134
realism   9, 40, 66, 72–3, 95
   the requirement of   40, 46, 80, 97–8, 133–4, 139
   and wishes   17, 24
reason, relation to desire   41, 52–4, 120–23
religious adherents, statistics   102
resignation   45, 87, 93–4, 136
resilience   1, 66
resurrection   111, 128
revolution   94–5, 98
Ricoeur, Paul   57, 81
Rudd, Kevin   93

salvation   7, 126
Santa Claus   21, 25, 39
Satan   61
science   90, 113, 120, 125, 134
second coming   100, 130, 137
selfishness   57
Seligman, Martin   8–9
Shade, Patrick   28–30, 35, 53
sin   116
Sisyphus, myth of   103, 112
slave trade   98
social contract   83
Socrates   107–9, 112, 120, 125, 135
South Africa   93, 131
Soviet Union   99
spiritual anxieties   102–7
spiritual enlightenment   112, 116, 130
Stalin   99
subjectivity   53–8, 60–63
suffering   116
Summa Theologica   4
supplication   36–9, 44–6, 67, 71, 95–6, 106, 133
   excess of   137
   in health care   79–80

Taj Mahal   114
technological brinkmanship in medicine   74
technology   90
temporality of hopes   49

Ten Commandments 112
theology 134
transcendence 107, 111, 126–7, 135
Tutu, Desmond 93

United Nations 87, 93
utopian thinking 98

values pluralism 59

Vanuatu 131
Vietnam War 97
virtue, defined 1
   Aristotle on 2–4

war 59–60, 131
wishes, compared to hope 16, 20–23
wishes defined 16